Development,
Demography, and
Family Decision-Making

**Brown University Studies
in Population and Development**

**Published in cooperation
with the Population Studies and Training Center
Brown University**

Editor
Calvin Goldscheider

Development, Demography, and Family Decision-Making

The Status of Women in Rural Java

Linda B. Williams

Routledge
Taylor & Francis Group

LONDON AND NEW YORK

First published 1990 by Westview Press, Inc.

Published 2018 by Routledge
52 Vanderbilt Avenue, New York, NY 10017
2 Park Square, Milton Park, Abingdon, Oxon OX14 4RN

Routledge is an imprint of the Taylor & Francis Group, an informa business

Library of Congress Cataloging-in-Publication Data
Williams, Linda B.
   Development, demography, and family decision-making: the status of
women in rural Java/Linda B. Williams.
     p.   cm.—(Brown University studies in population and
development)
   ISBN 0-8133-8020-0
   1. Women in rural development—Indonesia—Java.   2. Women—
Indonesia—Java—History.   3. Family demography—Indonesia—Java.
I. Title.   II. Series.
HQ1240.5.I5W55   1990
305.42′09598′2—dc20
                                                                        90-32924
                                                                        CIP

ISBN 13: 978-0-367-01568-8 (hbk)

ISBN 13: 978-0-367-16555-0 (pbk)

Contents

viii

Figures and Tables

FIGURES

TABLES

ix

Foreword

The shift toward the small nuclear family and the emergence of new roles for women have been among the conspicuous changes accompanying economic development and social modernization. As the power of the extended family waned, the control exercised by others over the status and roles of women and over their decision-making declined as well. Cumulative comparative and historical evidence has documented that along with increases in educational levels and the greater mobility of persons to new expanding economic opportunities, the size of families declines, individual responsibilities for making decisions about marriage increases, and, in turn, the roles of women and men in and out of marriage change. Altered gender roles do not necessarily imply "improvement" in the status of women vis-a-vis men; the shift toward greater "equality" between men and women is by no means uniform. Despite increases in societal level economic opportunities, the growth in women's educational attainment and occupational achievement, and the shift away from traditional sources of status and authority, the status of women within households and families, and in relationship to their husbands, does not always increase.

The importance of changing autonomy for women in the reduction of control over women's lives by the extended family in the process of development raises questions about the linkages among these processes in developing nations. What is the relationship between the changing roles of women in society and the extent to which women are involved in the choices to marry? How do the demographic processes of migration affect the autonomy of women? How does autonomy affect fertility behavior and contraceptive use? These core issues are addressed systematically and in detail in this volume.

There is a growing recognition of the importance of changes in family and household structure as contexts for studying the determinants and consequences of demographic shifts in fertility and migration. Moreover, it has been increasingly argued that improving the status of women is an important policy direction in the attempt to facilitate the reduction of high fertility in developing nations. It has been clearly demonstrated that studies of migration in the rural areas of developing countries need to examine the role of women, not simply whether women migrate more than men, but how migration affects the status of women and what consequences migration has for autonomy and decision-making power.

Dr. Linda Williams's research is an innovative examination of these issues for one developing nation. She traces out the complex interactions among three critical processes--migration, fertility, and marriage--in a lucid and compelling analysis of rural areas in Central Java. She shows the contribution of women to the family economy in Indonesia, the activity of women in the labor force, and the control women have over household decisions. Her research focuses on the intergenerational dynamics involved in the marriage decision and the socio-demographic processes, especially migration, that influence the ability of women to control family decisions once they are married. She investigates the role of the extended family and the amount of contact maintained between the generations; and she tests directly the impact of women's autonomy on the use of contraception and fertility. This study of the linkages among marriage, female autonomy, migration, and fertility in one setting is an important contribution to the demography of developing countries and to the understanding of development issues, particularly the changing role of women and families.

Her research places these themes in the context of the relationship between population and development and the policies related to both processes. Moreover, she includes as an integral theme the examination of women in development processes. Her framework focuses on how women fare vis-a-vis other household or family members in making major household decisions. She carefully outlines the arguments that show that development processes may improve or weaken the status of women. She focuses in particular on the migration dimension. She convincingly argues against the view that the migration of women is insignificant and associational, particularly by showing how migration is related to the status of women.

Dr. Williams addresses these issues in the specific context of the Indonesian province of Central Java. As in the examination of demographic processes in general, transitional countries like Indonesia can provide some of the richest insights about changes in the status of women within the community as a whole as well as within families. The members of over 500 households were interviewed in four villages in rural Central Java, with a focus on women and their husbands. These originally collected data are a rich and unique source of information that probe in-depth issues of family decisions, the status of women, migration, fertility and contraceptive use.

Several major findings emerge from the detailed analysis of these data.

*Some of the major predictors of decision-making power associated with marriage are as expected--parental education, years of schooling particularly for women, and exposure to life in a large urban center. There is some evidence, inferred from age and marital duration data, that there have been significant increases over time in the decision-making power of women in rural areas of Central Java.

*Residential mobility after marriage increases the status of the wife within her household, suggesting that women gain influence with their husbands through residential mobility. However, relocation beyond the borders of their villages loosens ties with the social networks of women and their decision-making power suffers. Thus, there is a balance between autonomy and the networks that affect that status and power of women within the household. Migration at or after marriage and the amount of contact maintained with parents on both sides of the family influence the amount of control exercised by women over family decisions. The more input into the decision to marry, the more control exerted by them in later household decisions as well.

*Contrary to expectation, women with high levels of status within their households were less likely to have ever used any form of contraception. Dr. Williams suggests that this finding might reflect responses to the sometimes coercive family planning program in Indonesia--women with higher status might be better able to resist outside pressure. So autonomy may under certain conditions result in the greater receptivity of women to innovative forms of fertility control, while under other conditions the increasing autonomy of women's roles may result in the rejection of pressures from agencies to encourage contraceptive usage and fertility control.

Important policy questions are raised by the analysis, particularly the negative response of women to family planning programs and to the general normative climate of family intervention. These findings challenge some accepted programs in developing nations. The results of this study reinforce the importance of the study of family contexts and the autonomy of women in the contraceptive usage patterns and fertility of rural women. They also point to the value of linking migration and fertility analyses in the investigation of issues of female autonomy.

These and other detailed findings are carefully documented by Dr. Williams using the special survey that she designed and the data she collected. The data were gathered as part of a 1985 survey of households in rural Central Java, supported in part by a Ford Foundation grant to Brown University's Population Studies and Training Center. The survey was integrated into the fieldwork of another researcher who was examining issues of labor allocation and migration in these same rural areas. The results of that research project were reported in an earlier volume in our series--Philip Guest, *Labor Allocation and Rural Development: Migration in Four Javanese Villages* (Westview Press, 1989). Dr. Williams first presented the analysis of these data as part of her 1987 doctoral dissertation in the Department of Sociology at Brown University. Serving on her doctoral dissertation committee were Frances Kobrin Goldscheider, Chair; Alden Speare, Jr.; and Sidney Goldstein. This monograph represents a revision of that dissertation following a review by a committee of senior demographers at Brown University and an outside reviewer expert in the field.

This volume is one of several in the Brown University Studies in Population and Development series published by Westview Press that have focused on various aspects of migration in developing nations. It is the first to connect in a systematic way the status of women, the decision to marry, fertility, and migration. And it carries on the tradition of fieldwork in less developed nations as part of the training and research apprenticeship provided by the Population Studies and Training Center at Brown University.

In all, Dr. Williams has provided us with a carefully designed series of tests of some of the fundamental questions associated with population and development in developing nations. Her findings are not likely to be limited to the rural areas of Central Java but are applicable to large parts of the rural developing third world. Policy makers and planners as well as demographers and development experts, would benefit from a careful consideration of the implications of her analysis. Dr. Williams's research reminds us once again of the importance of family and women in population processes and development.

Calvin Goldscheider
Editor, Brown University Studies
in Population and Development

Preface

This manuscript has evolved over the course of several years, and a number of people deserve special recognition for their contributions along the way. First, I would like to thank Dr. Philip Guest for including me in what was originally his research project on household labor allocation. His help and advice were invaluable to me. In addition, I would especially like to thank Professor Frances Kobrin Goldscheider, who chaired my dissertation committee at Brown University. Without her initial support I would never have made it to Indonesia to participate in the fieldwork for this research and would probably not have written a dissertation on this topic at all. Her extremely helpful comments at every stage of the dissertation and her continued support have been greatly appreciated.

The other members of my committee, Professors Sidney Goldstein and Alden Speare, Jr., also deserve a great deal of credit and many thanks for their inputs into the dissertation. Each member of the committee contributed very different kinds of insights, and together they made the process both interesting and enjoyable. The variety of information they provided was one of the things I appreciated the most about working with my committee, and I consider myself very fortunate to have worked with all three of them.

I would like to express my appreciation to the Population Studies and Training Center and to the Ford Foundation for providing the financial backing that made the fieldwork possible. And I would very much like to thank Dr. Suharso and his staff at Leknas in Indonesia, both for their guidance and support, and for the extremely high quality of their work throughout our association with them. I learned a great deal from them about survey research, and they made working in Indonesia very pleasant for us. The skill and understanding of the interviewers they hired and the cooperation of the people in the villages we surveyed were also essential to the success of the project and were very much appreciated.

I would like to acknowledge the very useful comments of an outside reviewer, and I would like to thank Calvin Goldscheider for his help and encouragement in getting this manuscript published. In addition, I would like to thank Carol Walker for her help and patience in formatting the book, Betsy Gould for her editorial comments when it was still a dissertation, and Stephen Singer for his help in editing it when it reached later stages. Last, but certainly not least, I would like to thank my family and my friends at Brown and elsewhere for their support over the years.

Linda B. Williams

1

The Role of Women in
Socio-Economic Development

Research questions are frequently raised about the nature of the family as an entity, the types of relationships that exist among its members, and the associations between the family and society. Across cultures, the family has been essential to the foundation of the social structure, forming the basis for class hierarchies and bearing responsibility for the initial socialization of virtually all of society's members. As the process of diversification has begun to take hold in many parts of the world, the family has also served as a vital link between individuals and emerging institutions (Goode, 1982).

Over time, however, the collective elements involved in social and economic development have in turn precipitated substantial change in the form and function of the family as a unit. The extent to which this evolution has occurred varies widely, but Goode (1982) has outlined 14 elements that have been instrumental in most family transitions worldwide. These include decreasing matriliny, decreasing power and prestige of "corporate kin groups," declines in the prevalence of bride prices and dowries, a narrowing of the age difference between husbands and wives, decreasing control by parents of their children's choices in marriage partners, and increases in autonomy among women.

While all of these developments are important in their own right, the latter two are the focus of attention in this research. The first is of interest because, although much has been written about the timing of marriages in less developed countries (Dixon, 1971; Smith, 1980), and considerable information exists about the relative strength of inputs from the marriageable individual versus other family members in the selection of the spouse (Goode, 1963), few analyses have been conducted to determine which factors most influence the balance of decision-making power between those getting married and their families. Instead, the variables that determine whether marriageable individuals act relatively autonomously (with the betrothed playing the primary role in the marriage decision), or whether the decision is generally made under the direction of others in the

1

family or community, have remained largely unexplored in the literature.

Also neglected have been the factors that affect the extent to which women are able to control other central matters within the household. Because increased attention has recently focused on the importance of women's roles and statuses as both determinants and consequences of demographic change, the need to determine which social agents most enhance or detract from their overall status has become all the more pronounced.

In this research the analysis will focus first on the dynamics involved in the marriage decision, and then on how a number of social and demographic processes, especially migration, influence the ability of women to control family decisions once they are married. Ultimately, the impact of variations in levels of autonomy among women upon specific demographic outcomes will also be assessed. Before these issues can be analyzed in any depth, however, it is necessary to place them in a broader social context. Also included, therefore, is some discussion of how the roles and statuses of women appear to have been affected over time by the interrelated processes of population growth and socio-economic development.

In addition, because the issues raised in this research are fairly specific, involving the family dynamics surrounding decision-making and decision outcomes, questions as to whether or not, and if so to what extent, the topics investigated might be of interest to policy makers with a still wider focus, also warrant some attention. As a consequence, some of the issues most central to the debate about population growth and economic development are introduced in the following discussion, and some of the ways in which the topics explored in this study might be seen as part of the larger picture are delineated.

POPULATION AND DEVELOPMENT: AN OVERVIEW

The nature of the relationship between population growth and economic development is far from unambiguous. Questions surrounding that topic have generated sporadic and sometimes heated debate among scholars since the late 18th century, when Thomas Malthus first expressed concern about the impact of population growth on living standards. Malthus argued for the existence of a negative feedback mechanism between the two processes whereby 1) an increase in the standard of living would precipitate population growth (due largely to earlier first marriages), 2) that growth would result in diminishing returns to agricultural labor, and 3) the end product would be demographic as well as economic decline. "Population, when unchecked, increases in a geometrical ratio. Subsistence increases only in an arithmetical ratio. A slight acquaintance with numbers will shew the immensity of the first power in comparison of the second" (Malthus, 1959: 5, (originally published in 1798)).

His critics have included among others, Marx and Engels. According to Engels, "even if we assume that the increase of output associated with this increase of labor is not always proportionate to the latter, there still remains a third element - which the economists, however, never consider as important - namely, science, the progress of which is just as limitless and at least as rapid as that of population" (Engels, quoted in Meek, 1971: 26). Lenin concurred, noting that "the law of diminishing returns does not apply at all to cases in which technique is progressing and methods of production are changing; it has only an extremely relative and restricted application to cases in which technique remains unchanged" (Lenin, quoted in Meek, 1971: 26).

History ruled against Malthus in the context of Europe, as advances in technology and the institutional change that accompanied industrialization helped to ensure that some of his more dire predictions would not be realized. In addition, in spite of increases in the standard of living and decreases in mortality rates throughout much of the 19th and 20th centuries, population growth rates failed to take off during that period. Instead, between 1880 and 1910 fertility fell dramatically in a variety of social settings and under a wide range of social, demographic, and economic conditions. Once begun, the decline in fertility occurred both rapidly and irreversibly (van de Walle and Knodel, 1980), and as a consequence, the concern about population growth and debate about its relationship to economic development largely subsided for the next several decades.

Since the 1950s, however, interest in the relationships between the two processes has resurfaced. Wide income disparities between more developed and less developed nations have become acutely apparent, and although recent economic growth in the developing world has been impressive, particularly among middle income countries, those gains have very often been offset by the speed with which populations have grown. The result has been that increases in per capita income and overall standards of living in less developed countries (LDCs) have not kept pace with growth in the industrialized world, and rapid population growth has again come to be viewed by many as a detriment to development (Coale and Hoover, 1958; van der Tak et al., 1979; Merrick et al., 1986).

Within the developing countries themselves, the problems of rapid population growth have not been limited to industrializing sectors; they have often been particularly acute in agricultural sectors. Fertility is usually highest in rural areas and among the poorest families. As land is subdivided and subdivided again, the result tends to be either out-migration or more intensive farming of smaller and smaller plots. In the case of the latter "resources are spread too thin to allow for the 'investments' beyond sheer survival, such as education, which might help these families lift themselves out of poverty" (van der Tak et al., 1979: 21). Migration has thus frequently become the alternative of choice.

Migration is not without its own costs, however. The evidence increasingly suggests "that problems of population distribution and rural-to-urban migration are moving to the forefront of government concerns. Of 116 less developed countries surveyed by the United Nations in 1978, 94 percent expressed some degree of dissatisfaction with their population distribution patterns, and about 60 percent reported the patterns to be highly undesirable" (Goldscheider, 1983: 4). Because economic growth at the destination is frequently insufficient to keep pace with migration flows, the results often include unemployment, underemployment, housing shortages, and inadequate infrastructure. When urban labor markets are unable to absorb the influx of rural migrants, political, social, environmental and economic instability can arise. "It gives the poor the frustrating choice between growing rural poverty, as the per capita land base shrinks, or eking out a miserable urban livelihood" (Beier, 1976: 18).

Because scientific advances and the social environment enabled Europe to escape the economic and demographic downturns predicted by Malthus, however, there are a number of writers who claim that technology will also eradicate the population-related problems facing today's LDCs. Proponents of that view argue that, given time, the presence of markets will allow for the realignment of population, resources, and the environment. They maintain that although population growth may initially create imbalances, human ingenuity will again provide a correction. "Extra children will eventually cause more inventions than otherwise because of the greater 'need,' which, in turn, may force people to work harder to invent new ways to reduce work. (In paradise no one would have an incentive to invent anything)" (Simon, 1977: 201). If the correction does not take place, it is because markets are constrained and thus unable to stimulate sufficient innovation and entrepreneurship (Simon, 1981; Merrick et al., 1986).

Simon's view may be correct in the long run. In the meantime, however, the gaps that remain between rich and poor nations are considerable, and raising the living standards of those in the lower tier to a point at which they can approximate those in the industrialized world is presenting policy makers with a formidable challenge. In addition, it has become apparent that countries with higher per capita GNPs tend to be those with lower levels of fertility and higher life expectancies. And it is clear that high rates of population growth are associated with the exacerbation of inequitable distributions of income within countries, as well as with the deterioration of living standards among lower income groups (Birdsall, 1980).

Results from a recent report by the National Academy of Sciences (1986) indicate that when the other elements involved in production remain constant, population growth is likely to reduce the productivity of labor, lower wages in agriculture, and precipitate the depletion of renewable resources. In the long run, rapid population growth enhances income disparities by causing the returns to labor to fall in comparison to the returns from the other factors of production. On the micro level, couples who have many children are able to spend less per child on health, nutrition, and education, and as a consequence, children from larger families are frequently less healthy and less well educated than are those with fewer siblings. The prevention of future unwanted births should therefore improve the prospects for children within families among whom birth control is either not utilized or not utilized successfully (National

Research Council, 1986).

Given this background, it is not surprising that there is again a strong contingent who insist that "one of the principal requirements in most less developed countries is clearly the earliest possible reduction of high fertility rates" (van der Tak et al., 1979: 21). And it is not surprising that programs aimed at fertility decline have become a priority among many population pundits. To date, however, the approaches and emphases of such programs have varied considerably. For example, because of the range of cultural contexts that exist and the variety of philosophies that are espoused throughout the different regions of the world, the position of the United Nations Fund for Population Activities (UNFPA) has been that "neutrality, innovation and flexibility," must guide their policy initiatives. One of the Fund's central premises has been that "every nation has the sovereign right to determine its own population policy, and that individuals have the right to determine freely and voluntarily their family size" (Sadik, 1984: 2).

Although initially appealing, the potential for considerable conflict is inherent in this position, as it assumes that goals of nations and individuals coincide. When governments and individuals both desire fertility limitation, the establishment of strong family planning programs is an obvious first step toward satisfying both parties. In other cases, however, program decisions are more complicated. It has been argued, for example, that in situations in which reductions in fertility are desired by the policy makers but not by the general public, and when the fertility decisions made by couples begin to impose "external costs on other families - in overexploitation of common resources, congestion of public services, or contribution to a socially undesirable distribution of income - a case may be made for policies that go 'beyond family planning'" (National Research Council, 1986: 93). Such programs have been instituted in a variety of settings and have included more general campaigns to convince couples that lower family size norms are desirable, along with specific tax and incentive packages aimed at lowering individual fertility targets.

Whether or not governments and individuals agree, however, most policy makers now recognize that because the family is both "the basic unit of society and the primary socializing institution and transmitter of social norms" (Salas, 1984: 27), programs must address the needs of the family as a unit if they are to be successful. Those interested in fertility behavior are becoming increasingly aware of the "relevance of family systems and changing familial roles" (Oppong, 1984: 332), and particularly the evolving roles of women within the family, for their research and for policy outcomes.

Because interest in the grassroots actors has developed relatively recently, the processes by which the social position of women can be improved within both the family and society remain primarily a matter of speculation. It is clear, however, that the constraints and discrimination women face in education, employment, training programs, credit opportunities, and community life in general restrict their power, limit the resources available to them within the context of the family, and "strengthen the cultural pressures on women to define themselves as mothers" (Safilios-Rothschild, 1982: 328). It is also apparent that especially in societies characterized by strict gender stratification, women frequently must rely upon the birth of sons for security, power, and prestige (Oppong, 1984), and that this situation is aggravated because "there is considerable pressure, sometimes subtle, sometimes direct, to remain in this niche" (Salas, 1979: 221).

Policy makers interested in fertility reduction have therefore concluded that raising the status of women within developing societies is essential if they are to be successful in limiting population growth. In fact, it is now commonly argued that "little can be accomplished in the population fields without the active involvement and full participation of women" (Salas, 1979: 223). As a consequence, it is increasingly important to determine which factors most clearly define, limit, or enhance the social position of women within both the family and society.

THE ISSUES IN CONTEXT

In this research, these subjects are addressed in the context of the Indonesian province of Central Java. Java is an appropriate setting for a number of reasons. First, depending upon the source of information cited, the status of women within the country as a whole is listed as anywhere from quite high to very low. Whereas the Indonesian Department of Information (1968:5) claims, for example, that "the Indonesian Woman of Today has become the Equal of the Indonesian Man in every aspect, in every field," the 1988 "Country Rankings of the Status of Women" compiled by the Population Crisis Committee, place Indonesia among countries in which the status of women is "very poor." The position of women, both within the society and within the family, thus warrants further scrutiny.

Second, despite economic advances, thought by many to be the surest catalyst for curbing rapid population growth, Indonesia's population was increasing at a rate of over 2.0 percent as recently as 1985. Although government efforts aimed at improving access to contraception, and lowering family size preferences and ultimately fertility, have intensified dramatically over the years, the reproductive targets of individuals still remain at four or five children per couple throughout much of the country (McNicoll and Singarimbun, 1983).

In Java, population growth and population density have been considered serious problems for some time. As of 1980, roughly 62 percent of all Indonesians were living on that island, yet the land on which they were enumerated comprises less than 7 percent of the country's total area (Indonesia, Biro Pusat Statistik, 1982; Leiserson et al., 1980). If the status of women is linked to lower levels of fertility, the mechanisms through which that process might operate in Java should be examined.

Third, although individual concerns in Indonesia remain secondary to the needs of the family and the broader community, a certain amount of control has been shifting to individuals in decisions that affect them directly, including those surrounding marriage and the process of mate selection. Similar realignments in the balance of decision making power are occurring throughout much of the rest of the developing world, as children in a variety of social settings can now look forward to having considerable input into, if not total control over, decisions regarding the selection of their future husbands and wives. As is the case in much of the research on fertility and mortality transitions, it is the transitional countries like Indonesia that can provide some of the richest information about such changes in the marital decision making process and the current state of its evolution.

As a consequence, the first topic for analysis in this research involves variations in the level of control Indonesian parents are able to exercise over the choice of spouse for either a daughter or a son. The focus is on the intergenerational dynamics surrounding the marriage decision, as well as on gender differences in perceptions of power in the process of mate selection. These issues are important, not only in their own right as part of the family transition process, but also because a woman's input into the spousal selection process has been linked to her ability to control later household decisions as well (Conklin, 1981).

A number of predictors of women's autonomy are examined in the second stage of the analysis. Of particular interest is the impact of migration or residential mobility following marriage upon a woman's power to influence decision outcomes. Does the relocation of one spouse or the other, or both, affect the amount of input a woman has, compared to that of her husband and other household members, in determining important household matters? If so, is the timing of the move important? In addition, does the level of contact that is maintained with the parents on either side of the family affect this relationship?

In the final portion of this study, the importance of the wife's autonomy is assessed as it relates to specific outcomes, in this case, contraception and fertility. Overall, it is expected that changes in household residence that allow the couple to remove themselves from direct supervision and control by their parents should produce increases in status for women within the household (intra-household status), and that high levels of female intra-household status should result in increases in contraceptive use and decreases in overall fertility, compared to cases in which women's status within the household is very low.

It is also expected that women who have high extra-household status, or status compared to individuals outside the household, will be more apt to use contraception and have lower overall fertility than will those who have low extra-household status. Although migration is also likely to enhance status on this dimension, measures of this type of status are introduced primarily as controls; the connections between migration and extra-household status (Shaw, 1975), as well as those between extra-household status and fertility and contraception (United Nations Secretariat, 1984) are already well documented.

The goal of this research is not to investigate all of the determinants of family size or family planning utilization in Indonesia; nor is it intended as a study of migration and fertility. The analysis focuses on three specific topics: 1) the intergenerational dynamics involved in the marriage decision and how men and women fare differently in the process, 2) the continued influence of the extended family, often varying as the result of migration or residential mobility as well as by the amount of contact that is maintained with the parents on both sides of the family, upon a woman's position within the household after she is married, and 3) how these factors in turn affect contraceptive use and fertility, both of which are central to family and community life in Indonesia.

2

Women, Development, and Demographic Processes

In order to convey a sense of the context in which this research is framed, a number of questions must be addressed at the outset. For example, how has societal development in general affected the status of women, both within and outside the household? How has socio-economic development influenced migration behavior, and how, if at all, has migration in turn contributed to changes in female autonomy? A brief introduction to these issues is provided in this chapter.[1]

Before proceeding, however, it is necessary to clarify what is meant by the concept of "women's status". Although it is often discussed in the literature, critics argue that the term has been used too loosely, and that its meaning thus far has been "highly elusive" (Curtin, 1982:33), "ambiguous and poorly defined" (Powers, 1985:3). It has recently been suggested, however, that out of the "bewildering variety of specific terms and definitions... certain common threads" do emerge (Mason, 1985:7). Status definitions usually concentrate on aspects of inequality between the sexes, and the inequalities examined tend to be centered around power, prestige, and/or resource control or access (Mason, 1985).

In spite of these common features, status can still be viewed on more than one dimension (Safilios-Rothschild, 1982; Williams and Guest, 1985), and the dimensions do not always interact predictably (Powers, 1985). It is therefore necessary to clarify which dimension is going to be examined in each phase of this research. In the following overview of women and socioeconomic development, for example, the primary focus is on status on the broader level, status vis-a-vis others in the community or society. Status on that dimension must be addressed in order to understand the position of women in the overall economy and in the social order outside the household.

The extra-household status of women does differ, however, from status on the inter-personal level, often termed "power" (Safilios-Rothschild, 1982), and it is on that dimension of status that much of the remainder of this research will concentrate. Of primary concern is how women fare vis-a-vis other household or family members in making major household decisions. Determining the intra-household status of women is important because variations in distributions of power between household members have been found to affect decision outcomes, such as contraception and fertility, independent of other more commonly considered variables, including those that measure status on the broader dimension (Hull, 1981).

This chapter was designed to assess the ways in which recent history has produced changes in the status of women, both within and between households, and across cultures and levels of development.

WOMEN AND DEVELOPMENT

The exact nature of the effects of socioeconomic development on the social position of women has generated considerable debate in recent years. Although Goode (1982) has argued that development, and particularly industrialization, have historically been associated with expanding rights for women, he acknowledges that that view is highly controversial in feminist circles. He maintains, however, that "if we confine ourselves to the era preceding industrialization, and to the period of relatively moderate or advanced industrialization, the trend toward greater equality of women's status seems clear enough" (Goode, 1982:184).

There are numerous reasons why the initial stages of industrialization and economic development were often much less helpful to the overall position of women in society. In the early industrializing United States, for example, and particularly once reforms made factory work largely the domain of the adult male, wives remained at home doing household chores, many of which had been previously shared by their husbands. In rural areas, women of necessity took on additional agricultural work when men began earning incomes elsewhere. Over time, the lines between women's domestic work and men's work in offices and factories became increasingly distinct, and what were already noticeable gender differences were heightened by the fact that while male labor brought in cash incomes, women's work generally did not. As a result of "this differentially rewarded division of work, men came to be associated with the values of the industrial world - money, production, and power", while women "were linked to domestic values -love, nurturance, and self sacrifice..." (Lipman-Blumen, 1984:106).

The limitations on the economic power of women that characterized the early stages of economic development and industrialization were confined neither to the United States nor to the western world in general, however. Prior to the establishment of a cash economy in most settings, work tends to be viewed simply as work; although tasks may vary by gender, one job is generally not seen as more or less valuable than any other. With the introduction of new systems of rewards for different types of production, however, only certain workers receive compensation in cash for the work they do. As a result, their labor becomes more highly valued than that for which there are no cash payments, and those who bring home cash earnings become elevated in status above those who do not (Taylor, 1985).

In a variety of cultural, economic, and social settings, women have continually failed to share fully in the benefits of industrialization, despite the introduction of specific programs aimed ostensibly at improving overall conditions in the target areas. Women's issues per se have been largely neglected since colonial and early post-independence periods, and until recently very little if any attempt has been made to integrate women into the broader development picture. While policy-makers have focused considerable attention on rural improvements, growth in education, industrialization, and even in some cases on family planning, they have tended to have "little regard for the consequences of their policies on women" (Duley and Diduk, 1986:48-49).

As a result, many policies have proved to be disruptive to women in general. Programs enacted during colonization are thought to have been responsible for the introduction of new elements into the sexual division of labor that replaced more equitable relationships between men and women with the "marginalization of women in political decision-making spheres, in access and control over resources, and in jural rights and privileges" (Duley and Diduk, 1986:53). Extensive revisions in systems of land tenure and property rights were enacted that "significantly undermined traditional rights of access granted to women" (Duley and Diduk, 1986:54). In many instances, European colonialists issued land reform policies that resulted in the direct transfer of land ownership from women to men. Boserup (1970: 60) has argued that such reforms came about in Africa because "Europeans everywhere seem to have objected to the peculiar position of African women, that was so different from anything the Europeans were accustomed to."

The frequent inability of development policies to improve or even maintain the status of women has not been limited to colonial periods or post-independence regimes, however. Nor has it since been contained within social, geographical, political, or temporal boundaries. Planners from both socialist and capitalist states have often disregarded women's issues because they have seen requests for attention to such issues as "special pleading, a mechanical imitation of Western 'women's lib,' needlessly divisive and even antinationalistic" (Duley and Diduk, 1986:49). It is therefore not surprising that the insights that could have been gained from past experience are still not being used effectively to improve the situation of women in developing countries. In Korea, for example, the benefits from socioeconomic development are continuing to accrue disproportionately to men, despite the fact that women comprise a sizeable percentage of both urban and rural labor markets (Soon, 1977; Whyte and Whyte, 1982). This scenario remains common throughout much of Asia, and the rest of the developing world as well.

Although both Marxist and non-Marxist analysts have generally viewed the effects of the expansion of capitalism as gender-neutral, and although logically, the growth of capitalism should eventually "destroy the socially accepted and ideologically reinforced subordination of women," that process is failing to occur in many developing countries (Afshar, 1985: xii). As a result, and given the evidence contradicting Goode's contention that the situation of women demonstrably improves during moderate to advanced industrialization, many writers have now concluded that while the decline in women's status is particularly precipitous in the early stages of development, there also appears to be an overall decrease in status throughout "the process of national growth in most countries" (Loutfi, 1980:11).

In some ways Indonesia provides an example. According to Mather (1985), the subordination of the female population in Jakarta has been reinforced instead of reduced during the process of industrialization. Through cooperation with local "Islamic patriarchs" who serve as security guards and "labor agents" for the industries, Jakarta's industrial capital managers have been able to command a labor force that is both "cheap and docile." Women and younger employees are viewed as easily dominated, and the alliance between the capital managers and the village leaders has enabled the growing industries to hire and maintain these more malleable workers at comparatively low wages (Mather, 1985: 177).

In general, because industrialization and urbanization are so highly related, the problems women in developing countries face during one process are almost inseparably linked with those that occur as a result of the other. For a variety of reasons the numerous rural to urban moves that take place as urbanization occurs usually involve resettlement from an agricultural to an industrial economy. These moves have been argued to produce an additional and critical dependence of women upon men (Afshar, 1985). Once in the city, potential jobs for women tend to be disproportionately few and far from where the migrants settle. Hours are inflexible and urban employment is frequently incompatible with childbearing and childrearing, as well as with traditional views about what the nature of women's work should be and where it should take place. According to some, the bottom line remains that employers tend to prefer to hire males anyway, and that training programs that are largely male-oriented often have to be completed before employment is even a possibility (Boserup, 1970; Duley and Diduk, 1986).

These problems are familiar to urban women throughout the developing world, as both supply and demand factors contribute to the persistent low status of the female population in those regions. On the supply side, constraints include social norms regarding the respectability and suitability of the work among women at various life cycle stages. Because they lack socially acceptable alternatives, women with children and no access to child care must frequently engage in low-wage employment activities that are done at home. On the demand side, there is the sexual division of labor: gender segregation by task and by "discrete areas of waged work" (Standing, 1985:233). Women's work involves lower skill levels, lower wage levels, less unionization, and therefore generally less satisfactory working conditions than is true in male dominated occupational categories (Standing, 1985).

The situations in Indonesia and Thailand provide a case in point. The disparities that exist between male and female labor force participation rates in both countries are a function of a number of the factors already cited: institutional segregation, lower human capital levels among women, and again, varying norms about the roles men and women are expected to play. As a consequence, female migrants are much more apt to enter the service economy than are males, while men are more likely to end up in positions in sales or government administration (Smith, 1981).

In most developing countries, accelerated population growth and urbanization have combined to create abundant surplus labor that the new capital-intensive industries have been unable to absorb. The result has been "the development of a highly heterogeneous labour force and the systematic exclusion of large groups of the population from certain occupational opportunities" (Jelin, 1982: 254). Because demand for labor is limited, both men and women face potential unemployment or underemployment, but because of the perception that women's "domestic responsibilities will prevent them from being effective workers" (Jelin, 1982: 254), they are commonly excluded from the most desirable jobs.

Taken together, these examples demonstrate that despite the obvious increases in opportunities for women that become available during the process of socioeconomic development, the overall status of women need not approach that of men even in societies that have moved beyond the initial stages of industrialization and development in general. Whether the primary focus is on industry or the agricultural sector or both, many writers now view "development" per se as far from a panacea for Third World women. In fact, there exists a vocal constituency for the view that the varied problems associated with low status among women in developing countries are not simply the result "of forgetting to include women in development plans, or of assuming that they will always benefit from measures aimed at men. There is also positive discrimination against development for women" (Ware, 1981:11; see also Jelin, 1982).

In drawing upon Boserup's (1970) scheme of three separate stages of societal evolution, with three matching status levels for women at each stage, Ware (1981) has presented some additional insights about the nature of the relationship between the position of women within the social system and the various processes involved in socioeconomic development, particularly as it relates to agriculture.

In Boserup's first stage, the population is sparsely settled, cultivation is shifting, and women tend to be in charge of agricultural production. At the second level, populations become more concentrated, plow agriculture is introduced, and men become responsible for the majority of the farming tasks. In the third stage, both men and women work hard on intensively farmed irrigated plots. According to Boserup, the overall status of women tends to be lower at the second stage of the process than at either the first or the third.

Ware (1981:21) has suggested that if Boserup's view is correct "the impact of development upon women's status would [therefore] depend to a great extent on the exact point in the three-stage progression at which modern development began." At the first level, women are significant contributors to the overall economy. At the second, their contributions to production become less important, they become increasingly confined to domestic activities, and their status falls. Ultimately, however, Ware appears to agree with Goode; with "industrialization, in the long run, women re-emerge out of the domestic sphere and make their contribution to the general economy" (Ware, 1981:24).

Ware's contention is that many of the shortcomings of development policies to date have been the result of to their proclivity for confining women to the "second, agricultural stage, even when men have been moving into the industrial stage" (Ware, 1981:24). Such policy outcomes are particularly ironic since so many development programs have as a stated objective the will to slow population growth; yet it is the women in the second agricultural stage who have the highest fertility. Essentially, the roles and statuses of women in the first and third stages of Boserup's scheme can be partially defined through activities other than childbearing and childrearing, while those in the second stage rely on reproduction as their primary function.

In Indonesia the total fertility rate is still high, at 4.4 (Population Reference Bureau, 1984), yet the women in many parts of the country, including the portion of Central Java that is the focus of this research, appear to have moved beyond the second agricultural stage and into the third. Much of the land in agriculture is now irrigated, and both men and women are actively involved in agricultural production. If Ware and Boserup are correct, the status of women in Java should therefore be higher than that of women from regions still in the second stage of agricultural evolution.

Other factors are certainly involved in the determination of women's status, however, many of which are also related to social evolution and economic development. Anker (1982: 32) has discussed some of the more important of these, noting that the prescribed rules governing the behavior of women can be deemphasized and their overall status probably enhanced under conditions "where family members have been exposed to new ideas and new ways of life, such as occurs as a result of migration and formal education, and where social structure is less cohesive..." These issues, with particular emphasis on the relationship between migration and the roles and statuses of women, are examined in more detail below.

WOMEN AND MIGRATION

Although much has been written about other consequences of migration, including the impact on the sending area (Connell et al., 1976; Lipton, 1982), effects on the receiving area (Findley, 1977; Yap, 1976), and the adjustments of the migrants themselves (Goldscheider, 1983; Martine,

1979), relatively little attention has been given to the specific impact of migration on women. Given what has been thought to be the nature of most migration streams, especially those covering longer distances (Ravenstein, 1885; Shryock, 1964), the focus of most migration research has instead tended to rest on the male. Ware (1981:142) contends that while in some areas female migration "actually constitutes a majority of all migratory moves," such moves are still largely ignored. She has argued that this is because female migration has been considered unimportant in general, that writers have seen female movements as primarily related to marriage and thus insignificant economically, and that since many of these moves are from one rural area to another, instead of to an urban center, they have been deemphasized in the face of current attention to what are seen as the more pressing problems of urbanization.

In addition, much of the literature that does exist on women and migration "has been written largely from a male perspective" (Hafkin and Bay, 1976:1), with the idea being that the main elements of interest in female migration are simply mirror images of the same components of male migration. It has been argued that especially in societies characterized by patrilineal and patrilocal social systems, the movement of a woman to a new place of residence tends to be nothing more than a reflection of her association with her household or family (Connell et al., 1976). According to Little (1973:17), "the men followed the money and the women followed the men." Until recently, therefore, investigations into the separate determinants and consequences of female migration have been considered redundant and of insufficient interest to justify separate analyses (Thadani and Todaro, 1979).

Our understanding of different patterns, causes, and outcomes of female migration at last appears to be on the rise, but this recognition is very late in coming. Thadani and Todaro (1979) maintain that the existence of basic differences between male and female migration behavior should have been evident as early as 1966, when Lee's general migration model was introduced. Given Lee's (1966) insights, the "potential differences between male and female migrants at least as regards intervening obstacles and personal factors" should have been obvious (Thadani and Todaro, 1979:1).

Among the variables that help to determine the extent of these differences are political, economic, and socio-cultural factors that can, at times, allow or encourage male migration, while discouraging or prohibiting autonomous or even associational migration among women (Connell, 1984; Thadani and Todaro, 1984). Although extreme examples of such restrictions are becoming less and less common, their continued existence does provide insights into the origins of the "male bias" that has been prevalent in the migration literature to date.

In Iran, for example, particularly among the lower classes, access to information and modern sector opportunities is extremely unequally distributed between males and females. Migrants to Teheran are generally single men seeking employment, or other males accompanied by their often illiterate wives, daughters, and other female family members. Autonomous female migration is not encouraged. Since a man's honor depends to a great extent upon the virtue of the women in his household, the interactions of those women with non-kin males are severely restricted. Travel is closely regulated, and women who accompany or follow males to Teheran are often not allowed to travel beyond the boundaries of their neighborhoods. Those who do venture outside such boundaries may generally go only under supervision (Bauer, 1984). The limitations placed on female mobility, along with their highly deficient educational attainment, combine to make procurement of employment outside the household very unlikely. When the broad picture is examined, it therefore becomes clear that although migration in Iran is a viable mechanism through which males seeking economic advancement can attain their goals, it is a much less realistic option for women.

If one focuses specifically on conditions at the origin or the destination in a particular country, instead of on broader-based societal variables, it is also apparent that different settings frequently produce quite different migration responses in males and females. In some situations, the division of labor at the origin can be such that the members of one sex hold much greater responsibility for production than do those of the other. The non-producers are then often more likely than the active producers to move away. In some instances, agricultural innovations have been responsible for altering the production process disproportionately, making the labor of either males or females superfluous, while leaving the demand for the other relatively unchanged.

Stivens (1985) has noted, for example, that among rice cultivators in Malaysia, tractors have basically replaced male labor once needed for hoeing. Rice farming, which has long been considered to be primarily women's work anyway, is now increasingly being left in the hands of the female labor force. Male labor, no longer essential for cultivation, has become not only freer to seek opportunities elsewhere, but has often had of necessity to do so. As a consequence, although out-migration is now growing in popularity among young women, it was initially utilized as an adaptive strategy among men, who in most cases still comprise the bulk of rural-urban migration streams.

Under other conditions, women are more likely than men to move out. For example, until 1970 males in Tanzania traditionally outnumbered females in comprising migration streams to the capital city. Since then, however, women have been found to outnumber men (Sabot, 1979). Bryceson (1985) has suggested that the increase in the proportion of female migrants to Dar es Salaam may be due at least in part to a dramatic shift in the balance between the pros and the cons for women of remaining in the rural areas; at present, the push factors appear to be affecting females disproportionately. A young woman's livelihood is far less secure in her village than is that of a young man, and her "traditional access to the land and means of production is basically limited to usufruct rights conditional on [her] marital status" (Bryceson, 1985:141). As a consequence, many girls and women now migrate to the city in order to escape uncertain positions in the village economy.

Because varying conditions at the origins often induce quite different migration responses from males and females, it would seem logical that the same should hold when different destination pull factors are examined, and indeed, in many instances that does appear to be the case. Fields (1979) has demonstrated how complicated the scenario may in fact be, even in situations in which surface appearances suggest very little complexity. He has found that while females in Colombia are only slightly more likely than males to be lifetime migrants, they are much more responsive to economic pulls; however, when wage differentials are examined "both in an absolute and in a relative sense, men in Colombia have more to gain from ... migration than do women" (Fields, 1979: 261). Thus, although women migrate with less to induce them to do so, men are subject to greater pulls. The result is a levelling out of the two migration rates, and the creation of the misleading impression that there is little of note to distinguish female and male migration behavior in that country.

It is clear that whether conditions at the origin, destination, or in the society as a whole are examined, men and women can exhibit either very different or very similar migration responses depending upon the stimuli present; the migration of women does not simply mirror that of men. Separate analyses of female migration are therefore certainly warranted, even where autonomous, economically motivated migration among women is rare.

In fact, associational female migration may be of particular interest, as many of the most intriguing questions pertaining to these moves remain unanswered. For example, does a couple's move away from their parents and other social contacts change the relationship between the two spouses? Does it alter the processes through which major household decisions are made? Although some attention has recently begun to focus on the general topic of women and migration (see for example, International Migration Review, 1984; Fawcett, 1984), data about the effects of migration upon the status of women within the household remain sketchy.

Out of the studies that have been done on women and migration, no clear consensus has arisen as to which women move, why they move, or what impact their moves have upon their lives. This is also true of research into what becomes of the women who remain in the rural origins while their husbands migrate out. Instead, specific information as to who the ideal-typical female migrant (or stayer) in the developing world might be is often quite contradictory. In fact, the literature reviewed here suggests that women with widely divergent background characteristics are all likely to move if the appropriate circumstances present themselves.

Who Are the Women Who Migrate?

In one of the more comprehensive studies of the characteristics of female migrants in the Third World, data from 40 countries were examined (Youssef et al., 1979). The results suggest that the majority of women move either as mid-to-late adolescents, when in their early twenties, or when aged 50 or above. (Similar findings have also been reported by de Oliveira and Garcia, 1984). Women who migrate from rural places to cities are generally single, but those going in the opposite direction tend to do so in association with their husbands. Women over 50 years of age, a large proportion of whom are widowed, divorced, or separated, move both to and among cities, and in some areas single pregnant women are apt to comprise another part of rural-urban streams. However, single women, pregnant or not, are not likely to become return migrants once in the city (Castro et al., 1978). Given the findings of these writers, it appears that the women who move from the country to the city tend to be those who, due to their youth, have not yet established conjugal or economic ties in their places of origin, or those who, due to their advancing ages, have had such ties severed.

Some support for this pattern has been offered by .Ranney and Kossoudji (1983). According to their study of Mexican migrants to the United States, most women move either when they are quite young or much older, while those in their prime childbearing years generally stay behind in Mexico. Arizpe's (1981) study of internal migration from two rural Mexican villages has provided further evidence of the pervasiveness of migration among unattached women, but that study did not focus on women at both ends of the bi-modal age distribution. Instead, it concentrated on women who leave for Mexico City while in their early to mid-teens. Those women generally go as part of a family strategy to improve the economic well-being of the group, work for several years, and then return to the rural areas in their late teens or early twenties to raise a family.

In Malaysia, Khoo and Pirie (1984) found that 44.5 percent of the women who moved from rural to urban areas did so between the ages of 10 and 19. In addition, according to Piampiti (1984), most of the women who migrated to Bangkok from four selected rural villages moved when they were young adults, generally between the ages of 15 and 24. Eighty percent moved when they were single, although the percentage of married migrants did increase with age (Piampiti, 1984).

Recent research in Pakistan lends support to the bimodal age pattern of migration, but introduces some mixed evidence concerning trends in migration by marital status. According to Shah (1984), roughly 60 percent of the women included in her study moved when they were less than 25 years of age, although older single and divorced women (ages 45 and above) moved in relatively large numbers as well. Young single women generally did not move alone. Shah has estimated that approximately ten percent of all single women had migrated at some time; yet among single women aged 45 and above, about 64 percent had done so. Overall, divorced women were more likely to move than either married or widowed women, but of the women who had moved since 1965, 68 percent were married. Thus, although older single and divorced women comprise large portions of the migration streams in Pakistan, married women appear to be in the majority.

In India, the characteristics of the women who migrate vary by region. More females migrate in the north than in the south, but migrants in the south are more likely to be widowed or divorced than are those in the north. It has been argued that in the wealthier states, fewer women with severed family ties are forced to move because of economic necessity (A.M. Singh, 1984).

The evidence presented thus far suggests that while it may be possible to argue for a general age pattern of female migration, the data on marital status do not lend themselves readily to statements about who the ideal-typical female migrant might be. Evidence concerning the general economic position of the standard female migrant is also mixed, although certain patterns are discernible. While some writers argue that male migration (or migration that is not gender-specific) occurs primarily among both the most wealthy and the poorest households (Mazur, 1984; Chaudhury, 1978), others claim that it is those in the second and fourth wealth quintiles who are more apt to move (Connell et al., 1976). Although those authors do not deal specifically with female migration, women's associational moves may be covered in their analyses, at least for those in the upper strata. For the others, resources may determine whether or not the wife is given the option of accompanying her husband, togetherness often being "a luxury beyond reach for the very poor" (Ware, 1981:147).

As a rule, the literature concerning the migration of women in the Third World probably best supports the contentions of Connell et al. (1976); whether the move is autonomous or associational, it is not the very poor who are the most apt to move. Although a great many migrants come from lower-class families, at least some resources are generally required in order to finance their moves. In their study of Thailand, for example, Lightfoot et al. (1983) found that most migrants tend to be those with enough wherewithal to gather information about their destinations and eventually cover the costs of relocation. Arnold and Piampiti (1984) agree, noting that migrants to Bangkok generally come from provinces to which at least some of the benefits of development have accrued, while the poorest rural dwellers are much less likely to move.

The educational attainment of the ideal-typical female migrant has also been debated. Although higher learning, in and of itself, has frequently been found to be an important determinant of migration (Goldstein, 1973; Sabot, 1979), Youssef et al. (1979: 4) have asserted that their data fail to substantiate that finding "insofar as women are concerned." It is possible that this is because, relative to those who move autonomously in search of employment or advanced degrees, many of the women who move associationally do not require the most selective characteristics to accomplish the goals of their moves.

Despite evidence to the contrary, however, female migrants in developing countries do tend to be relatively well-educated. For example, although 22.3 percent of the female migrants in one study of Malaysia reported having had no formal schooling at all, the educational attainment of the migrants as a group compared favorably with that of the women in the general population. Both urban and rural non-movers were more apt to report having had absolutely no formal education than were the migrants themselves, and the migrants were more apt than either group of non-migrants to have completed some years of primary school. The only category in which the migrants had less education than either group of non-migrants was that measuring completion of secondary education. Urban stayers were found to be more likely than in-migrants to have completed a high school degree. Otherwise, the migrants in that study of Malaysia appeared to be better educated than non-migrants across education categories (Khoo and Pirie, 1984).

Elsewhere the amount of schooling completed by female migrants generally falls somewhere between that of urban and rural stayers. (See, for example, Eviota and Smith (1984)). The bulk of available evidence thus suggests that there is at least a certain amount of educational selectivity among female migrants. Such findings have been reported in Kenya (Knotts, 1979), Chile (Herold, 1979), Lesotho (Murray, 1981), Sierra Leone (Byerlee et al., 1977) and Zambia (Chilivumbo, 1985).

Even in countries in which women attain very little schooling, migrants appear to surpass non-migrants on education indicators. For example, although both migrant and non-migrant women in Pakistan are often completely illiterate, women who are multiple movers clearly have the edge in education over women who do not move at all. Shah (1984) has estimated that while 89 percent of female nonmovers in that country are illiterate, "only" 62 percent of female multiple movers have completed no schooling. Indeed, the association been migration and education holds even when age and marital status are controlled (Shah, 1984).

Finally, the level of education and the destination of the migrant are often related. Eviota and Smith (1984) have found, for example, that in the Philippines the women with the most schooling tend to be those most likely to move to a metropolitan area. Women who are relatively well educated, but who have had noticeably less schooling than their metro-bound counterparts, are apt to gravitate toward other urban centers, while the women with the least education generally stay in the rural areas.

Although numerous exceptions may certainly be cited, the association between educational attainment and migration appears to be stronger than either the relationship between migration and wealth, or between migration and marital status.

Why Do They Go?

Just as many of the questions concerning which women migrate have only begun to be addressed, information about why they move also remains inconclusive. In general, the reasons cited for female migration may be roughly divided into two groups: the economic, and the personal or social. Moves classified as economic include those related to finding or upgrading jobs, education, or income. Moves classified as personal or social include marriage migration, moves to attain greater independence, and associational moves. In many cases, categories within or between groups of economic and social motivations for migration may, of course, overlap.

In a recent review of the literature on women and migration, movers motivated by the search for employment were found to outnumber those moving for any other reason. As a rule, studies in which economic influences were cited as determining women's moves also outnumbered those in which women claimed to have moved for personal or social reasons (Findley and Williams, 1987). This was the case both within and across regions of the developing world, and it runs counter to the arguments of those who contend that women's moves are much more commonly social or personal than economic in nature.

On the other hand, associational moves were found to be the second most commonly cited moves among women in Asia and Africa, as well as among those moving from less developed to more developed countries; and they were only slightly less important among women from Latin America, the Caribbean, and the South Pacific. Marriage migration was ranked third in importance in Asia and Africa, a finding that was again roughly reflected in the other three regions (Findley and Williams, 1987).

Whatever the primary cause, the migration decision is an extremely complicated one, often involving more than one motivating factor, and involving them to varying degrees. Evidence from Malaysia provides an interesting case in point. Historically, the reasons for women's migration in that country were almost exclusively associational. When women moved it was either to be with their families or to marry. Otherwise they were expected to remain in the rural areas where they would presumably stay out of trouble, remain virtuous, and provide agricultural and household labor. Parents thought that if girls were to migrate to the city without supervision they would go astray and subsequently have trouble when they entered the marriage market. At the same time, there were virtually no jobs for any but the most highly educated young single women in the urban centers (Khoo and Pirie, 1984).

Recent developments in both urban and rural sectors have begun to produce significant changes, however. New labor-saving technology now allows girls to stay out of agriculture and in school longer than was previously possible, and if they are able to get enough education in the rural areas, they may consider continuing their schooling in the city. In some cases they are also able to attain the skills necessary for formal sector employment (Khoo and Pirie, 1984).

At the same time, girls in the rural areas now see local traditions being challenged by the spread of modernization, and many of them have begun to move to the city to escape the restrictions of the countryside. When they go, they go seeking both greater individual freedom and economic advancement. Although others would prefer to stay and work in rural locales, many of them also feel compelled to accept work in an urban center because no viable alternatives exist for them in their places of origin. The motivation for that group is therefore more economic than social in nature (Ariffin, 1984).

In Thailand, push and pull factors have also combined to influence the migration process. There, associational considerations and potential employment constitute the strongest pulls, while poverty, droughts, and off-season unemployment constitute the pushes (Arnold and Piampiti, 1984). As in the case of Malaysia, as rural traditions are being challenged, levels of education rise, and women's participation in the non-agricultural labor force begins to increase, migration to urban areas increases as well. Inadequate schooling and employment opportunities, along with unsatisfactory living conditions in the rural areas, provide a further impetus for rural out-migration (Piampiti, 1984).

Throughout the developing world, those who move and particularly those who move as part of a family strategy, often have little to say in making the final migration decision. In Korea, for example, many young girls are sent to Seoul after primary school or junior high school; some are sent to get additional schooling in the city, with the idea being that they will eventually make more money as a result of that investment, while others are sent into the job market immediately. According to Huang (1984), migrants who have some control over the decisions regarding their moves claim to go in search of improved skills, to find out more about life in the city, to get away from life in the village (especially the difficult agricultural work), or to escape parental controls. Whatever their stated objectives, however, most still go under parental constraints, as many are sent to live with relatives who are expected to keep an eye on them.

The situation in Indonesia is very similar (Hugo, 1981). There, parents and other family members have considerable input into the migration decisions affecting both females and males, although control over daughters is particularly strict. Most moves are undertaken to improve the general well-being of the group, and the families are expected to provide adequate funds to help the migrants get started. As is the case elsewhere, wealthier families are better able to finance moves covering longer distances and longer durations, and as a consequence, they tend to receive a higher rate of return on their investment.

Given the information presented to this point, it is clear that those who view the migration of women as generally insignificant and largely associational are apt to underestimate what is potentially a very complex process. More attention to the general topic of women and migration is therefore certainly warranted. One of the most central questions of this research has yet to be addressed, however; that is, how is migration related to the status of women, particularly the status of women within the household?

Migration and Status

One relatively early attempt to transcend the view that female migration merely reflects the movement of males, was undertaken by Thadani and Todaro (1979). While their approach was innovative, their conclusions may also be considered controversial in some circles. They argued that while men migrate in search of higher education or more prestigious employment, thereby enhancing their social status within the community, "an appropriate marriage to an upwardly mobile man may be an alternative or additional approach in pursuit of the same goal for women" (Thadani and Todaro, 1979:2).

Although the type of status being sought by the women in the Thadani and Todaro study is status on the extra-household or community level, other researchers have since developed an interest in the subject and discussed the possible impact of migration upon women's status within the household. Ware (1981) has noted, for example, that enhanced intra-household status may be one logical outcome of migration. She has argued that in patrilineal and patrilocal societies, a move away from the husband's family may aid the wife by severing ties with in-laws among whom all resources are controlled by older men. Without such a move "young brides are in a singularly powerless position because they are strangers in their husbands' families" (Ware, 1981:163).

A move away from the extended family is thought to give the couple the opportunity to develop a more intimate, and perhaps a more egalitarian relationship than would otherwise be possible. Ware (1981) contends that female migrants should be able to play a greater role in family decision-making processes than should non-migrants, and that "the greater participation of migrant women in economic tasks and the public sphere leads to the development of complex networks of communications and politicization" (Ware, 1981:172).

Support for this view has been offered by Conklin (1981). He has found that migration in India significantly augments women's capacity to control decision-making processes. This is true even when urban versus rural residence is controlled. He has argued that "a wife on her own, away from her husband's relatives, is better able to bargain for and receive more power than would otherwise be the case" (Conklin, 1981:17). Warner et al. (1986:123) have added that when patrilateral systems of residence and descent are examined, women are apt to have much less marital power than is true under other residence systems; "a woman typically becomes a de facto member of her husband's kin group upon marriage. That group acquires the rights to her reproductive capacities, since her children will belong to her husband's group."

Whyte's (1978) research is among that referenced by Warner et al.

(1986). According to Whyte, women in nuclear households are likely to exercise much more power within a marriage than are women from extended families. "The fact that extended families include a number of adults of each gender leads to or allows a fairly rigid sexual division of labor" (Warner et al., 1986:122). In nuclear households, on the other hand, there are fewer people available to substitute in and perform the roles of the key players. As a result, when a move is made away from the extended family, the wife becomes critically important to the survival of the household, and her power in making major household decisions increases accordingly.

Finally, Youssef et al. (1979:123) assert that one "important result of migration is the weakening of traditional family structures" and that family fragmentation and "the emergence of new family structures" are likely outcomes of the migration process. Goldscheider (1984) concurs, arguing that "one of the key changes which migration brings about...is the removal from the family in the place of origin of total control over resources and status" (Goldscheider, 1984:11). In the long run, a move may also "facilitate the separation of economic from family structures and allow them to be realigned" (Goldscheider, 1984:11).

Although some writers clearly view the association between migration and women's status as strong and positive, not all are as optimistic. Mueller (1983:280), for example, has argued that migration away from family ties "may deprive some women of a reliable source of support in societies where kinship obligations are normally strong." She maintains that "poverty and unemployment as well as urbanization and modernization" all play a role in the erosion of kin networks (Mueller, 1983:280). If a woman's residential relocation after marriage is of a sufficient distance to prove disruptive to her support networks, the move itself may not only fail to improve her status within the household, but it may cause her to feel even more powerless than she would have felt had she stayed right in her parents' home.

As is true of the other migrant characteristics that have been discussed, the association between migration and the status of women remains incompletely specified. The nature of that relationship thus warrants additional consideration, and is analysed in the following chapters.

STATUS, CONTRACEPTION, AND FERTILITY

Also of interest is the association between the status of women within the household, their contraceptive use, and the number of children they eventually have. As was discussed in the introductory chapter, it is now commonly argued that major reductions in fertility can be achieved in currently developing countries by improving the status of the women in those areas. Recognizing that a woman's status may be conceptualized on at least two levels, this research focuses primarily on status within households, and secondarily on status between women of different households, in attempting to predict contraceptive use and fertility. In both cases, the decision outcomes provide a means of operationally testing the decision-making processes of interest.

In studying intra-household status, contraception, and fertility behavior, the position of the woman is compared to that of her partner in the decision-making unit; essentially, the ability of either actor to influence the eventual decision is thought to depend upon the relative status of the two partners (Knodel and Van de Walle, 1979). In recent analyses, more egalitarian relationships have been argued to yield higher levels of contraception than those in which the wife must generally defer to her husband (Mason, 1971). Dyson and Moore (1983) conclude, for example, that not only is a woman's autonomy within the household important for fertility control, but it is "probably the single most important element in comprehending India's demographic situation" as a whole (Dyson and Moore, 1983:54).

Hogan et al. (1985) have found that Thai women who adhere to more modern views about the importance of egalitarian relationships between males and females within the household "have significantly lower rates of parity progression" than do more traditional women (Hogan et al., 1985:28). They contend that this is due in large part to lower desired family sizes and higher rates of contraceptive use among the more liberated women. These effects are also net of "family modernity," and are particularly strong at the extreme ends of the scale measuring the level of sexual liberation among the women surveyed.

One factor that tends to be ignored in studies of within-household status and fertility, is the importance of at least the potential for conflicting interests of the two partners. Without conflict, much of the discussion pertaining to power and fertility outcomes becomes irrelevant. Youssef (1982) cites several other assumptions inherent in contraceptive research that can make the investigations problematic. For example, it is assumed that there is the desire to limit fertility rather than to enhance it, that women wish to adopt contraception but that the major barrier is an unwilling husband, and that a joint decision must be made before the woman can control her fertility. In the case of the latter assumption, differential resource control should obviously play a role in areas in which contraception is not free, and the ability of either partner to carry out a strategy without the knowledge of the other must certainly come into play as well. (See also Beckman (1983)). As a consequence, differences between the fertility preferences of husbands and wives are also examined in this research.

Fortunately, examining the role of women's status on the second dimension, status which can be measured vis-a-vis others in the community in enhancing fertility control does not involve as many restrictive assumptions. It has been argued that higher status women are more likely to attempt to regulate their fertility because they acquire aspirations for goods other than children (Dixon, 1975), and that they are more likely to do so effectively because they have the knowledge with which to implement their desires (Curtin, 1982). The education, occupation, household income, and general socioeconomic status of women usually figure prominently in analyses on this topic.

Education is probably the most frequently cited indicator of female status on either dimension, and has been shown to inversely affect fertility via a number of mechanisms. For example, it has been found to exert a negative influence on infant and child mortality, to positively affect the ages at which women marry, and to increase the likelihood that contraception will be used (Cochrane, 1979). In addition, women with high levels of education are often better able to gain access to resources and knowledge than can their less educated counterparts, and can consequently enhance their autonomy within the family unit (Mason, 1985). Caldwell (1980) is among those who stress the importance of schooling in influencing fertility levels. His view is that as education becomes widespread and modernization proceeds, a couple's basic needs and economic security should become divorced from high fertility, and fertility control should then become a matter of joint utility for the two partners.

In cases in which an income is earned by the wife, and in which she is allowed at least some control over that money, differential resource control within the family should no longer be a factor limiting access to contraception. Furthermore, unlike women from the lower socio-economic strata, those in the upper or middle classes should not "have to rely on reproduction, the one unique gender-related asset of women, in order to diminish their powerlessness and alienation" Safilios-Rothschild (1982:121).

These variables are all intricately related. Where development has proceeded the furthest, and where women have access to education and the cash economy, the expectation is that their aspirations for goods other than children and activities other than childbearing will be more pronounced, and they will be better able to act on their desires than will women without similar access. In addition, the influence of extended kin on the household should be reduced as development proceeds and families become increasingly nucleated.

SUMMARY

Whereas many writers have viewed industrialization and socioeconomic development in general as likely to enhance the overall status of women, both within the household and within society as a whole, considerable evidence to the contrary has been discussed in the literature. Although awareness of the importance of women's issues in social evolution has at last begun to grow, serious concern over these issues has arisen only recently. In this chapter, issues pertaining to the association between the social position of women and varying levels of socio-economic development have been introduced, and some of the possible links between development, migration, and the roles and statuses of women alluded to. How the status of women might in turn affect contraception and fertility outcomes has also been briefly discussed. In the chapter that follows, an attempt is made to place these and other related issues in the context of rural Central Java.

NOTES

1. It is important to recognize that the definition of "development" varies from author to author. No single definition for the term exists in the literature, and it is virtually certain that a number of the works referenced here have utilized different conceptualizations. Ware (1981:7) has noted that the common ingredients to a definition of development usually entail "growth, progress, the achievement of potential" and the availability of and ability to use human and physical raw materials. In addition, there is generally a distinction drawn between rich and poor nations. In spite of those similarities, however, different writers continue to assign different countries to different development categories.

The indicators chosen to measure development also vary from study to study. Although per capita gross national product (GNP) and gross domestic product (GDP) are among the measures most commonly utilized, there are well known problems inherent in both. Such problems include the failure of each indicator to capture nonmonetized productive activities in developing countries, their inability to incorporate elements of living standards such as education, nutrition, and health, and their failure to measure income distribution within countries. When comparing rich and poor countries, the first of these shortcomings would tend to overstate the relative advantage of the more developed nations, while the second (and probably the third) would bias the measure in favor of the developing world. Although some authors have attempted to adjust for these problems through the adoption of such measures as Morris's Physical Quality of Life Index (PQLI), per capita GNP is still among the measures used most frequently to compare levels of development between countries.

3

The Indonesian Context

In this chapter, some of the issues raised in Chapters 1 and 2 are examined in the context of Indonesia. For example, what is the role of women in Indonesian society? How were female roles viewed in the past, and how, if at all, have they changed over time? Do the patterns of residential mobility and parental contact after marriage influence the status of women within Javanese households? Finally, how might the answers to these questions be useful in the analysis of individual contraception and fertility patterns in the context of rural Central Java?

INDONESIA'S POPULATION

Figure 3.1 provides a sense of the size and location of Java in relation to the rest of Indonesia.

Indonesia is the fifth most populous country in the world. According to estimates from the Population Reference Bureau the total population had reached 177.4 million as of 1988. The country is inhabited by over 300 different ethnic groups, each with its own cultural identity, and each one defined within relatively distinct geographical boundaries. In spite of the country's ethnic diversity, however, 87.5 percent of the people in the various ethnic groups adhere to a single religion, Islam (Suparlan and Sigit, 1980). This research focuses on one of the predominantly Muslim groups, the ethnic Javanese of Central Java.

Some basic data on the population size and density in Java and Indonesia as a whole[1] are presented in Table 3.1. As the data suggest, among Indonesia's most distinctive demographic features is the uneven distribution of its population and the extreme density of the population in some parts of the country. For example, depending upon the source of data utilized, estimates of the population density in Java for 1980 range between 620 and 680 people per square kilometer.

TABLE 3.1:   TOTAL POPULATION (in millions) AND POPULA-
TION DENSITY IN INDONESIA (1920-1971)

	Indonesia as a Whole		Java and Madura	
YEAR	Population	Density/sq.km	Population	Density/sq.km
1920	49.3	24	35.0	259
1930	60.8	30	41.7	310
1961	97.0	48	63.0	468
1971	118.5	58	76.1	565
1980	146.8	72	91.2*	676*

Table constructed from data from Suparlan and Sigit (1980:
16), and from information from the 1980 Census (Indonesia,
Biro Pusat Statistik); * indicates data for Java only.

As a consequence, availability of land has increasingly become a factor
affecting where a newly married couple might live, how many children they
might have once they are settled, and the labor force allocation of the
family as a unit. As land availability becomes more and more restricted,
couples may find it difficult to establish independent households soon after
they marry. They may have to live with one or the other set of parents or
move a considerable distance away. If the plot on which they eventually
settle is very small, they may have fewer children than they would
otherwise have, or expect some to migrate when they get old enough to
work.

Several studies have demonstrated how unequally distributed and
generally inaccessible land in Indonesia can be (Mangkuprawira, 1981).
White (1976) has found, for example, that while 6 percent of the families in
Kali Loro own 50 percent of the sawah (land used in the production of wet
rice), 40 percent own fewer than 0.2 hectares, (or the approximate amount
of land needed to produce adequate rice for the average household for the
year), and 37 percent own none at all. Similarly, Hull (1976) has found
that among households in Maguwoharjo, 70 percent of the families involved
in agriculture own or have access to fewer than 0.2 hectares. Given limited
access to land, many women have had to supplement household incomes by
seeking outside employment, and have entered the cash economy as a
result (Mangkuprawira, 1981).

31

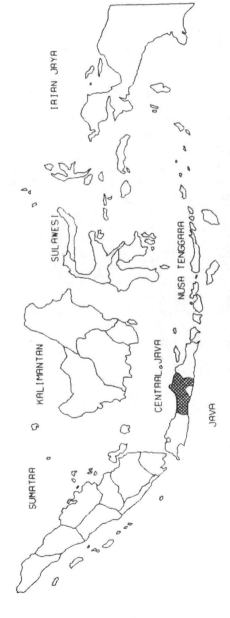

FIGURE 3.1: MAP OF INDONESIA: MAJOR ISLAND GROUPS, PROVINCES, AND CENTRAL JAVA

WOMEN, WORK, AND STATUS

According to Mangkuprawira (1981), while most women in Indonesia undertake wage work outside the home only when economic necessity demands it, necessity has become the rule rather than the exception in most parts of the country. Although the bulk of the earnings of women in rural areas comes from agricultural production, uneven land distribution, high population density, and lack of industrial growth make maintaining a subsistence living (roughly 1200 kgs. of rice per year) difficult. In Java and elsewhere, women have long worked side by side with men in the fields playing the dual roles of housewife and wage earner (Mangkuprawira, 1981).

Unfortunately, as is true throughout much of the developing world, precise measurement of women's work presents a formidable challenge in Indonesia. In a recent review by Hugo et al. (1987), the authors argue that changing definitions of labor force participation have rendered available data unsuitable for measuring temporal changes in female rates. Because women's activities are so often "on the borderline between 'economic' and 'noneconomic'" and because women "are also more likely to work part time, erratically or seasonally in those activities... conventions about how to treat such activities can have an important bearing on the size of the female labour force measured by censuses or surveys" (Hugo et al., 1987: 251). Regional differences, on the other hand, can be more fruitfully analyzed and the data suggest that rates "in the Javanese areas are always well above the Indonesian average" (Hugo et al., 1987:252).

By most definitions the amount of land owned by the household and the proportion of time women spend engaged in income earning activities are inversely correlated, as women from households with large landholdings are generally not compelled to supplement the family income through outside employment. As a consequence, the more land the household controls, the higher the proportion of time women will designate for housework. Women from poorer households spend more time engaged in wage labor, and thus have fewer hours to allocate to domestic work (or to leisure activities).

On the other hand, although much of the agricultural work is seasonal and the hours spent engaged in agricultural production decline from December to March among all socioeconomic groups, the hours spent on household work vary little across seasons. As a rule, whatever the season, middle-class women spend more time on domestic work and less time in the labor force engaged in "directly productive activities" than do the women from the bottom strata. Across income groups, women with many children are also more apt to be involved in wage work than are those with fewer children. The more children there are, the more money is needed to support the family, and the greater the likelihood that some of the children will be old enough to look after their younger siblings while their mother works (Mangkuprawira, 1981).

Much of the directly productive work that is done by Javanese women is in wet rice cultivation. Although historically, that type of work has been highly labor intensive, the recent growth of new technologies in agricultural production has been labor-replacing. The advent of sickle methods has lowered demand for laborers during the harvest, while the mechanization of hulling and milling has brought about a similar decline in the demand for hand-pounding labor. Since the majority of handpounding and harvest work has traditionally been done by women, both new technologies have been particularly detrimental to their position in the labor force (Mangkuprawira, 1981).

For this and other reasons, returns to female labor in rural Java are generally low. Given the seasonality of women's agricultural work, much of their time is spent in occupations that offer little payoff. Because "of low returns for labor of the 'open-access' occupations and the limited access of the others, there is no single occupation in which women can earn much more than their own support throughout the year... [In addition,] hardly any rural woman manages to secure employment for 365 days a year and thus female incomes remain well below the poverty line" (Mangkuprawira, 1981:103; White, 1976).

The Sexual Division of Labor

Within the household, men do an estimated 62 percent of the agricultural work, yet women work an average of three hours more per day than do their husbands. Although men spend more time in directly productive tasks than do their wives (7.9 hours per day for men and 5.9 hours for women), women contribute more hours to activities that are "indirectly productive" (White, 1976; Mangkuprawira, 1981). Because women have access to fewer job opportunities and face greater constraints in the job market, their participation in directly productive work can be less than half that of men. This is especially likely to be the case where infant mortality rates and child/woman ratios are high (Mangkuprawira, 1981; Connell and Lipton, 1977).[2]

According to Geertz (1961), there are several possible combinations of husband-wife labor allocation within the Indonesian household. In one scenario, the man works and his wife stays home. In another, husbands and wives work together in agriculture as a team; although there is some sex-specificity as to the tasks undertaken by each spouse, many of their activities are interchangeable. In the third case, the husband and wife may again be viewed as a team, but in business, often as market traders. Finally, the husband may provide greater input into directly productive tasks, while his wife does something that is less "directly productive" at home.

Of the four possible combinations, it appears that it is most common for husbands and wives in Central Java to work together as a team, generally in agriculture, in order to support a family (Koentjaraningrat, 1967). Further support may thus be offered for the idea that Central

Javanese women may be in Boserup's (1970) third phase of agricultural development. While certain tasks are gender-specific, it does not appear that particular jobs are more highly valued than others.

Women's Status Within the Household

Not only do couples work together as part of a family survival strategy, they also cooperate considerably in making household decisions. According to Bangun (1981: 129), they not only "share economic activities, mainly agricultural and handicraft, they also discuss all their problems." Women are allowed at least an equal say, if not more, into decisions regarding how important household matters will be settled, especially in decisions about the control of household resources (Mangkuprawira, 1981; Geertz, 1961). Middle-class women in particular have been found to engage in detailed discussions about birth control methods and family size ideals with their husbands (Hull, 1976).

> In family gatherings the wife has a say in the matter under discussion, no law can prevent her from becoming *mamak*, and she is often *kepala waris*.[3] She manages her own possessions during the marriage..., and this in complete agreement with the *fikh*.[4] She is greatly respected, especially when she is old... Modern influences and individualization have [at last] opened up large breaches in the traditionally closed way of life (Vreede-de Stuers, 1960:28).

The ability of Indonesian couples to communicate and to discuss family matters is not without exception, however. Many women from the lower end of the socioeconomic scale never discuss topics such as contraception or family size preferences with their husbands. It has been argued that this is because they are too busy with daily activities and because they are socially isolated from organizations through which they could learn about and discuss family planning options (Mangkuprawira, 1981; Hull, 1976). For the most part, however, the decision-making power of women within the Indonesian family appears to be relatively high on a range of issues.

Women's Status in Society in Historical Perspective

The social position of women within the society as a whole is less clear-cut. Some writers contend that the status of women in the broader community is relatively high, especially when compared to that of women in other Islamic countries (Bangun, 1981). Others maintain, however, that the power of Indonesian women does not extend far beyond the walls of their own households.

In public and political affairs..., the village women do not play a leading role, and, although female landholders have the same voting rights as men, they are usually not interested in such matters, preferring to send sons or brothers as their representatives to village meetings (Koentjaraningrat, 1967:260-261).

Deciding which elements within the historical context have most directed the course of the evolution of women's social position has also been a matter of much debate. According to governmental reports, women have played important roles in Indonesian political life since before the introduction of the Islamic religion and Dutch colonial rule. "The history and literature of Indonesia show how high the position and how great the role were of women during the periods of kingdoms in Indonesia" (Indonesia, Department of Information, 1968:7). Under *adat*, or the customary law of the various regions of the country, the position of women within society was viewed as no different from that of men, and women were frequently found in positions of military and political leadership.

Some writers have argued that it was with the strengthening of Dutch rule and Islamic law that the status of women within the country began deteriorating. According to their view colonial policies were highly disruptive to the economy and the social structure in general, and the introduction of the Islamic religion, which has always officially "regarded women as socially inferior to men" (Vreede-de Stuers, 1960: 46), played a major role in undermining the social position of women. Although it has been argued that women in Indonesia have suffered from fewer limitations than have those from cultures in which *purdah* is followed conscientiously, by the turn of the century the position of women within Indonesian society "had become anything but enviable" (Vreede-de Stuers, 1960:47).

On the other side of the argument are those who believe that rather than being detrimental, the introduction of Islamic law actually helped bring about improvements in the condition of women as individuals within Indonesian society. Proponents of this view argue that while *adat* allows for sexual equality in home and society, the needs of the individual still remain secondary compared to those of family and community. They contend that the introduction of Islamic law precipitated improvements in the situation of individuals (both male and female) by teaching them to "free themselves from the family group" (Vreede-de Stuers, 1960:41).

They acknowledge that the situation of women did deteriorate to a point at which women became inferior to men, but suggest that this was the result of a combination of factors, most of which were unrelated to the growth of Islam. The relaxation of traditional customs, the influx of modern ideology and social change,[5] as well as women's "ignorance of their rights according to the *fikh*" were all seen as contributing to the downturn in women's status (Vreede-de Stuers, 1960:41). While a certain amount of controversy remains as to which factors have been most responsible for determining the roles women are expected to play in the Indonesian family and society, it is clear that the two legal systems in Indonesia have been among the forces central to the process.

Women and Law

The *adat*, or customary law, governs all members of all religious groups in Indonesia, yet the majority of the population are Muslim, and so are also governed by the *fikh*. The distinctions between the two legal systems are sometimes tenuous, since a certain amount of overlap does exist, but as yet no uniform law has evolved. Attempts at codification have been recognized to be in the best interests of many groups, including women, since their behavior is governed by both sets of laws, but thus far little progress has been made. As a result,

> relationships within the group are currently determined by ancestral custom, the *adat* - the indivisible entity of unwritten prescriptions which law experts have a habit of differentiating into civil law, private law, matrimonial law, and law of succession; the indivisible whole that varies within the regions, the origins, and the beliefs, and that has evolved with time according to the vicissitudes of the social groups concerned (Vreede-de Stuers, 1960:21).

In essence, the *adat* affects the man or woman as a member of the society, rather than as an individual, although it has been argued that the distinction between the individual and the society member should not be exaggerated.

Within the *adat*, matrilineal, patrilineal, and bilineal social systems all operate. In Java, the bilineal system is most common. The children born to a couple thereby belong to both sides of the family, and both sons and daughters can inherit property. Among married couples, the "possessions inherited or acquired by either partner during the marriage, the *(gani-gini)*, become the common property to which they have equal rights" (Vreede-de Stuers, 1960:30). If the couple decides to separate, all possessions that were brought into the marriage by the man remain with his family, while those brought into the marriage by the woman remain with her side. Property acquired since marriage is split so that the wife receives one third of its value, while her husband receives two thirds (Koentjaraningrat, 1967).

According to the *adat*, marriage:

> is a ritual which symbolizes the passing from both the man's and the woman's state of celibacy to the marital one. From this interpretation arises, for example, the Javanese custom of changing the name on this occasion. The young man and girl who marry take a name new to both of them as a symbol of unity" (Vreede-de Stuers, 1960:33).

Like most aspects of life that are governed by *adat*, marriages are determined on the basis of what is considered to be good for the group. Marriage is an agreement between two families and young people may be denied direct input into the marriage decision. Although parents try to take their tastes into account, marriage is not seen as a means to make individuals happy (Ihromi et al., 1973). "Marriage becomes a duty, and spinsters are looked upon with contempt. A woman proves her true worth and comes into her full rights only on becoming wife and mother" (Vreede-de Stuers, 1960:31).

In some portions of the country, an individual must be married in order to take part in any major decisions that pertain to the family or community. In certain cases, only women with children are allowed an input, and in cases of strict patriarchy or matriarchy, both of which exist in Indonesia, only those with children of the appropriate gender can take part in such decisions (Ihromi et al., 1973). Much of Indonesian custom is thus functional and aimed directly at ensuring the continuation of the clan. As a result, it is not surprising that under both the *adat* and Islamic law, sterility is grounds for divorce (Vreede-de Stuers, 1960).

The extent to which the two legal systems agree is in fact considerable, as their roles in governing marriage customs provide a case in point. Under Islamic law, marriage is seen as an agreement "by means of which the husband gains certain rights over his wife, while she, in exchange, claims proper treatment" (Vreede-de Stuers, 1960). In theory their union constitutes a contract between two individuals and requires the consent of each. As is true under the *adat*, however, "in practice the group influences the choice, and the settlement of marriages is 'the family's business and not that of the future husband and wife'" (Gardet, 1954:250 cited in Vreede-de Stuers, 1960: 31). Also of interest is that customs such as forced marriages, polygamy, child marriages, and repudiation rights[6] that were initiated under *adat* before the introduction of the Muslim religion into Indonesia, are now frequently reinforced using Islamic law.[7]

On the whole, much of individual behavior before, during, and after marriage is regulated according to legal precepts. Under Islamic law the husband is bound to support his family of procreation. He must not "leave home for more than two years; is obliged, if he has several wives, to treat them equally; and must refrain from bad treatment which may lead to bodily harm" (Vreede-de Stuers, 1960:33). If the marriage eventually proves unsuccessful, however, a divorce may be awarded at the request of the husband without his wife's consent. Custody of non-infant children can be awarded to either spouse, but infants always remain with their mothers. Whatever the outcome of the custody decision, however, both parents remain responsible for the well-being of all children after a divorce (Koentjaraningrat, 1967).

In summary, there are specific laws governing a range of behavior throughout an Indonesian's lifetime. At times they are complementary, while at others they are contradictory, but there are no set rules specifying which will prevail in the case of a discrepancy. One of the primary interests of this research involves the customs surrounding entry into marriage. Under *adat*, the rules vary with the family system of the region in which they are enforced, and at times by urban versus rural residence. In Java, where bilateral systems are the norm, spousal selection is less strictly controlled than is the case in many other parts of Indonesia. As has been noted, however, members on both sides of the family do take part in the marriage decision, with the chosen spouse being one who is expected to strengthen the existing family (Ihromi et al., 1973).

Women and Employment Today

In spite of some of the restrictions placed on women by the legal systems in Indonesia, a fair body of evidence exists to support the views of those who argue that the social position of women is relatively high in Indonesia (Mangkuprawira, 1981; Bangun, 1981; Koentjaraningrat, 1967). According to Ihromi et al., (1973:32), women now play central roles not only in the economy of the household, but in that of the broader society as well. Women from all socioeconomic status groups are able to participate in "education and employment so that it is a common phenomenon that women have a job outside the household, namely in offices and factories, as physicians, lawyers, judges and even as engineers, in addition to their participation in social and political activities."

At the time of the 1980 Census, the highest proportion of women working in the urban labor market were employed in public service jobs (39 percent), followed closely by those in trade (33.6 percent), and those in the industrial/ manufacturing sector (14.6 percent). Among urban males, the same was true. A third had jobs in public services (33.3 percent), followed by those in trade (20.2 percent) and those in industry (13.4 percent).

Among women and men in rural parts of Indonesia, the proportions employed in different sectors of the economy were also comparable. Most (61.4 percent of the females and 67.3 percent of the males) were employed in agriculture. Among women, 15 percent were traders, 10.3 percent worked in the industrial/manufacturing sector, and 9.8 percent worked in public services. Service employment was slightly more common among rural males, with 10.8 percent holding jobs so designated, while 7.5 percent were working in trade and 5.8 percent in industry/manufacturing. Although these figures demonstrate nothing about the relative positions of men and women within these fields, they do indicate that contrary to some of the information presented in Chapter 2, women have at least been allowed access to the same sectors of the economy as have men.

Some basic data on female and male occupations are presented in Table 3.2. At the time of the 1980 Census, both men and women were more likely to work in agriculture than in any other sector of the economy, and both were less likely to be in management or administration than in any other occupational category. While men were more likely than women to be employed in production, transportation, or clerical and related work, women were more likely than men to hold jobs in sales or services. Finally, although in absolute numbers men filled the majority of positions as professionals and technical workers, as a percentage, women were slightly more apt to hold professional or technical jobs than were their male counterparts.

The Rise of the Women's Movement

Many of the improvements that have occurred in the employment picture to date are the result of long concerted efforts to bring about such changes, efforts that in some cases were initiated prior to 1900. Among the first to trigger the feminist movement in Indonesia was Raden Adjeng Kartini (1879-1904). Records of her communications with a Dutch woman, whom she recruited to be her correspondent through a Dutch feminist newspaper, have provided invaluable information about the social position of Indonesian women at the turn of the century. In one of her letters written in 1899, she explains:

> We girls, so far as education goes, fettered by our ancient traditions and conventions, have profited but little by these advantages.[8] It was a great crime against the customs of our land that we should be taught at all, and especially that we should leave the house to go to school. For the custom of our country forbade girls in the strongest manner ever to go outside of the house... When I reached the age of twelve, I was kept at home... I was locked up and cut off from all communication with the outside world, toward which I might never turn again save at the sight of a bridegroom, a stranger, an unknown man whom my parent would choose for me, and to whom I should be betrothed without my knowledge (quoted in Vreede-de Stuers, 1960:50-51).

Kartini's experience appears to have been typical of that of the other young girls of her day and of her social class. N.D. Sewojo, an instructor at Djokjakarta's Teachers' Training College, has described the situation of Javanese women in the four socioeconomic groups of the time as follows. First, daughters of poor villagers did not attend school. They worked in the fields, at selling produce, and on occasion at sewing. Their lives were difficult but they were allowed a certain amount of independence. Daughters of wealthy villagers were taught household chores and were married between the ages of 12 and 15. They too received no schooling. Once married, they worked in conjunction with their husbands in trade or in agriculture, and were generally treated well.

TABLE 3.2:   OCCUPATIONS OF INDONESIAN MEN AND WOMEN AS
OF 1980 CENSUS

Occupational Category	% Males Employed	% Females Employed
Professional/technical, and related	2.9	3.2
Management/ administrative	0.2	0.1
Clerical and related	4.8	1.5
Sales	10.1	18.7
Service	3.1	7.8
Farmers and agricultural workers	55.8	52.4
Production, transportation, and related	21.0	14.3
Others	0.9	0.2
Not Stated	1.2	1.8
Total	100.0	100.0

Daughters of the *santri* (religious teachers) did not receive formal education but were taught to recite the Koran at home. They were not married until around age 15 and tended to be held in high esteem by their spouses. Finally, daughters of the *priyayi* (noble civil servants), were allowed to attend some primary school, but only until the age of 12. After that they were forced to stay at home where they had many servants and lived very idle lives. They married when they were 15 or 16 and continued a life of inactivity and confinement. Child marriages were possible in all classes. The rationale behind the promotion of such unions was to "prevent a girl from choosing according to the dictates of her heart rather than reason" (Vreede-de Stuers, 1960:52). Not surprisingly, children were seen as being far more malleable than older individuals.

Although by 1900, 1200 desa (village) schools had been established, no public schools had as yet been made available to girls from the lower social classes in Indonesia. In an attempt to improve the situation of girls and women in her country, Kartini called for substantial increases in education for those from all socioeconomic groups. Her rationale was that education for girls was necessary, not so that women would compete with and threaten men, but so that they could do a better job of raising their families and producing high quality members of society. That theme was picked up and reiterated throughout the history of the women's movement in Indonesia. According to one government report:

> Indonesian feminism differs from Western feminism. The latter was mainly aimed at opposing the efforts of men, for the sake of the progress of the women... In Indonesia it was exclusively by way of educational efforts by women, and afterwards by way of ... [women's involvement in] large parties and associations, that the [women's] movement became the basis for the rise of national feelings of unity, of nationhood and in the resistance of Dutch and Japanese colonialism, so that in the end the situation was sufficiently ripe for the participation of women in the struggle for independence (Department of Information, 1968:11).

Women and Education

Data from recent censuses can be used to provide an idea of how far the campaign to improve educational standards among Indonesian woman has since progressed. The data indicate that while female literacy levels in the nation as a whole increased from 22 to 32 percent between 1961 and 1971, most Indonesian women were thus still illiterate at the time of the 1971 Census. By 1980 that was no longer the case; 63.6 percent of the female population over age 10 were then classified as literate. While literacy rates are still lower for women than for men in Indonesia, (as male literacy was over 80 percent by the time of the 1980 Census), the overall position of women appears to have improved substantially in recent years.

In Java, higher proportions of both men and women are literate than is true nationwide. Among those over age ten, roughly 75 percent of females and 90 percent of the males were literate by the time of the 1980 enumeration.

To enhance educational opportunities for women, the Community Education Division has instituted 48 courses, including literacy, in informal education programs aimed specifically at the female population. It has been the view of policy makers that improvements in education should increase the number of job opportunities available to women, improve "self-expression and independence," raise "knowledge and skills, to a new place in a new social order," and provide a "motivating force for change" (Mangkuprawira, 1981:91).

The more specific objectives of the division's programs have not always followed the traditional western model, however. For example, among its primary goals is "educating women in their roles as home-makers" (Mangkuprawira, 1981:91). Also emphasized is information about nutrition and health. Because it is commonly believed that inadequate education, health, and nutritional practices not only interfere with living standards and the general well-being of individuals, but also decrease their productivity and therefore their ability to earn adequate support for themselves, attempts to improve women's knowledge in each of these areas have been viewed as crucial in recent policy initiatives (Bangun, 1981).

In addition to courses on health and hygiene, women are also taught basic skills such as sewing (Mangkuprawira, 1981). Although increasing education of this sort is thought by some to be one way to improve the status of women in Indonesia, many women still fail to attend available classes (Bangun, 1981). This is in large part because the classes require not only time, but money. Women who are fully employed generally lack the time, and those who are not generally lack the money. The barriers to success are thus interrelated; low education precludes better employment,[9] while the lack of financial resources precludes increases in educational attainment.

For example, many of the women who might be interested in the sewing classes live only at subsistence levels and are unable to afford the cloth needed to participate in the classes. Those who are able to take part are often left without access to credit upon completion of their courses, and as a result the classes prove to be of little practical benefit to them. Similarly, the literacy programs are often designed inappropriately for the populations at which they are targeted. Many of the teaching materials used to convey basic reading and writing skills to village women are neither simple enough, nor applicable enough in terms of the topics discussed in the readings, to be of use to those in a rural setting (Bangun, 1981).

Finally, it has been found that village women are still reluctant to speak out in classes in which village men are present, and they are frequently uncomfortable when being taught by males (Epstein, 1981). If education is to be an effective tool for raising the status of women in Indonesian society, these problems will have to be recognized and addressed.

The problems of rural education are not limited to the adult female population, however. The schooling of children is frequently neglected as well. The reasons for this are often financial, although it is also common for relatively wealthy families to take their children out of school early. In such cases the school facilities may be inadequate or the parents may not sufficiently understand the benefits of education for their children. In other cases, parents are fully aware of the potential benefits of school for their children, but fear that if the children become educated they will become disenchanted with life as peasant farmers and take up employment elsewhere (Koentjaraningrat, 1967).

RESIDENCE PATTERNS

Regardless of the level of schooling completed by a female in Indonesia, it is expected that she will eventually marry and raise a family. One of the central questions addressed in this research is whether or not the couple's choice of residence upon marriage then influences the amount of control each spouse is able to exert in making major household decisions. Accounts vary somewhat as to where Javanese couples do tend to live when they get married, but there appear to be several common options.

According to Koentjaraningrat (1967), most couples hope eventually to form their own households. Since many marry at very early ages, however, they often must live with one or the other set of parents for a few years (usually three to five) before relocating to a place of their own. In such cases, the couple is more likely to settle with the parents of the wife than with those of her husband, out of deference to the feelings of the wife. Once the couple becomes independent, they are again more likely to establish their new home close to that of the wife's parents, than to move to another village or to a home at a considerable distance away within the same village. In fact, it is not uncommon for a married daughter to continue to live with her parents throughout her adult life, eventually inheriting their home (Koentjaraningrat, 1967).

Nag et al. (1980) agree that upon marriage, the couple traditionally spends at least some time in the home of the bride's parents, but note that the amount of time spent there can range from one night to a number of years. They have also found that when a couple eventually moves to a separate residence, they tend either to settle close to the home of the husband's parents or to move in with them. Because the woman generally marries a man who lives near the home of her own family, she will remain close enough to her parents to maintain contact with them and to assist as when they get older, even if she becomes part of her in-laws' household (Nag et al., 1980).[10]

There is general agreement that although there are a number of possibilities as to where the couple will finally locate, the ideal is the establishment of a separate nuclear household. (See also Jay, 1969). Even when the couple forms its own household, however, both spouses maintain close ties with their own parents. Possibly as a consequence, the parents continue to participate in family decisions well after the new household is established (Vreede-de Stuers, 1960:30).

THE VALUE OF CHILDREN

Among the most important of those decisions are the ones involving childbearing. As is true in other developing countries, the expected economic returns from having children have encouraged relatively high levels of fertility in Indonesia. The economic benefits expected to accrue to parents are generally manifested in the form of additional labor power and the provision of security in old age, and Indonesian children appear to be conscientious providers of both. For example, among Javanese 15 to 19 year-olds, males contribute an average of 7.9 hours per day to directly and indirectly productive activities, while their sisters each contribute over ten hours.

The data presented in Table 3.3 demonstrate that even very young children make substantial contributions to the functioning household economy. By the time they are between the ages of 12 and 14, girls average over eight hours of labor a day, while their brothers contribute close to five. Even boys and girls between the ages of six and eight provide over three hours of labor each day. Javanese girls in that age group have been estimated to spend 1.7 hours per day looking after younger siblings, so small children do not always constitute a drain on their mothers' time. Nag et al. (1980:256-257) have found, for example, that in "only two of the 20 Javanese households do mothers spend more time than other household members in child care; in the majority of cases, it is the elder siblings who do the majority of this work."

TABLE 3.3:   JAVANESE DAILY WORK INPUTS BY SEX AND AGE*

Type of Activity by Gender	Average Daily Work Inputs (Hours) by Age							
	6-8	9-11	12-14	15-19	20-29	30-39	40-49	50+
Household Maintenance:								
Male	1.9	1.4	1.5	0.3	0.4	1.5	0.5	0.3
Female	2.3	2.4	4.0	3.7	4.9	6.7	4.5	3.8
Directly Productive:								
Male	1.7	1.7	3.2	7.6	8.3	7.9	8.2	7.0
Female	1.2	3.0	4.7	6.5	7.1	5.2	6.0	4.6
Total:								
Male	3.6	3.1	4.7	7.9	8.7	9.4	8.7	7.3
Female	3.5	5.4	8.7	10.2	12.0	11.9	10.5	8.4

*Table was retabulated from data presented in Nag et al., (1980: 251-252).

TABLE 3.4: AVERAGE TIME SPENT IN SCHOOL AS A PERCENT-
AGE OF AVERAGE TIME SPENT IN ALL WORK FOR CHILDREN OF
VARIOUS AGE GROUPS

| Gender | Hours by Age Groups | | | |
	6-8	9-11	12-14	15+
Boys	73	112	56	2
Girls	76	53	20	0

Data obtained from Nag et al., (1980:256).

As has been noted, Javanese women spend more time engaged in indirectly productive activities than do their husbands, and that pattern holds across all age groups. Except among the youngest working children, girls and women in all age groups spend more time engaged in total work activities than do their male counterparts. Conversely, males in most age categories spend more hours per day in directly productive activities than do girls or women, except when they are between the ages of 9 and 14. Nag et al. (1980:257) suggest that that is because "girls of these age groups participate in a major way in handicrafts, trade, and wage labor, whereas the boys... participate in a major way only in animal care." While boys in these age ranges spend virtually no time in the preparation of food for the household, girls in the corresponding age group spend an average of 1.3 hours each day.

Not only are certain tasks gender-specific, but differences in labor allocation are also determined by the varying amounts of time girls and boys spend in school. As the data in Table 3.4 demonstrate, boys spend a higher proportion of their time in school than do girls, relative to their other work. This is particularly apparent when they are between the ages of 9 and 14; again, those are the only ages during which female participation in directly productive activities exceeds that of males. Variation in the labor inputs of boys and girls is thus not only the result of the sexual division of labor, but it is also related to differences in the amount of time children of both genders spend in school.

Children from large families reportedly work more hours than do those

from smaller households. Nag et al. (1980) have argued that this may be
either because younger children are inspired to work hard by older siblings,
or because older children are able to engage in directly productive work
once the others are able to take over their household chores. Whatever the
reason, the increased labor contributed by children from larger families
allows substantial benefits to accrue to those families. As a rule, larger
families are more successful economically than are smaller ones. The

**TABLE 3.5: TOTAL FERTILITY RATES IN INDONESIA AND JAVA:
FINDINGS FROM 1971 AND 1980 CENSUS DATA**

Location	1967-1970	1980	Percent Change
Indonesia	5.61	4.27	-24
Java	5.26	3.89	-26
Jakarta	5.18	3.94	-24
West Java	5.94	4.47	-25
Central Java	5.33	4.08	-23
Yogyakarta	4.76	3.25	-32
East Java	4.72	3.27	-37

Data from Hull and Hull, 1980.

**TABLE 3.6: CONTRACEPTIVE PREVALENCE IN JAVA AND INDO-
NESIA AS A WHOLE (1984)**

Location	Women 15-44 (1000s)	% Using F.P. Method
Indonesia	24,469	57.3
Java		
DKI Jakarta	1,115	53.9
West Java	4,932	56.5
Central Java	4,162	64.3
DI Yogyakarta	397	75.3
East Java	5,119	71.6

Data from Hull and Hull (1984).

number of labor inputs children contribute to a household is found to be significantly correlated with the ratio of the household's income to its expenditures on food, and is independent of the amount of land the family controls for wet-rice production (Nag et al., 1980).

Overall, the average total daily labor inputs of males and females are 8.7 and 11.1 hours respectively. If only directly productive activities are considered, the average is eight hours for males and six for females. According to Nag et al. (1980:262), it is therefore "erroneous to categorize the people doing so much work as unemployed or underemployed, even though the economic returns from many occupations are indeed quite low." They have argued that opportunities abound outside wet and dry rice cultivation, and that participation in such opportunities depends less on availability of land and capital than on the demand for the labor, the demand for the product that the labor would produce, and the amount of livestock and grass that are available within the rural villages.

As a consequence, whenever the local economic situation is favorable, each "household can obtain income from many occupations, in direct (not declining) proportion to the amount of labor that the household can provide" (Nag et al., 1980:263). Increasing family size should therefore result in increases in overall household productivity, whether the increase in labor power results from reproduction or recruitment of additional household members. As a result, Nag et al. (1980) contend that as long as additional family members are still able to find productive activities through which to raise the level of family well-being, Java should not be considered "overpopulated".

Although individuals from other parts of the developing world may prefer sons to daughters, in Java that does not appear to be the case. Parents rely fairly equally on boys and girls, and so tend not to express a preference for one or the other. In addition to the substantial amounts of household labor children of both genders provide, this may be due, at least in part, to the flexibility of postmarriage residence patterns described earlier. Since both sons and daughters tend to live close enough to their parents to provide them with long term assistance, all children are highly valued. ·

Indonesian parents have an average of four children. Of these, 1.5 generally move away and 2.5 stay in the village. In the unlikely event that all four children leave, their children may come to the village to care for, or be cared for by the grandparents. If a couple has no children, they are likely to try to adopt in order to ensure that they will receive some assistance when they get older. Again, neither gender is preferred (Nag et al., 1980).

In summary, most couples expect to have several children, both because they are a good source of productive labor, and because they provide old age security. Whether or not age and marital duration are controlled, the family size preferences of women and men tend to be similar; each prefer an average of four or five children (McNicoll and Singarimbun, 1983; Williams, 1988). In Java large families have traditionally been desirable, not only because children are economic assets, but because they have intrinsic value and are generally considered a blessing (Koentjaraningrat, 1967).

FAMILY PLANNING IN INDONESIA

Despite the fact that most Indonesians prefer large families, the Indonesian government has been disenchanted for some time with the country's high rate of population growth. Family planning as a national policy was introduced as part of the Mother and Child Health Centers as early as 1957, although official commitment was initially very limited. By the middle of the 1960s Indonesia had a crude birth rate of 45/1000, and the annual population growth rate between 1961 and 1971 was 2.1 percent (Hull and Hull, 1984). As a consequence, by 1967 the new leadership began to focus attention on the need for family planning, and in 1968 the National Family Planning Institute, later renamed the National Family Planning Coordinating Board (the Badan Koordinasi Keluarga Berencana Nasional, or BKKBN), was founded. The overriding objective of the government's policy at that time was "population management for socioeconomic prosperity," through the increased use of contraception and through the creation of "a common national outlook positive to family planning" (Suparlan and Sigit, 1980:8).

Central to the program philosophy was that the provision of information, individual motivation, and continuous reinforcement were essential in order for a successful family planning effort to take hold. Of primary importance in getting the official message to targeted individuals were increases in education for women, along with the introduction of population education for all students enrolled in middle schools, high schools, and teacher training schools. The organization had as an initial goal to cut the 1971 total fertility rate of 5.2 in half by the year 2000, and to increase the number of contraceptors to one quarter of all potential users by 1979 (Teachman, 1979).

With strong support from the government, the BKKBN began utilizing the already existing health infrastructure to reach the rural population. Soon thereafter, the training of field workers for "house-to-house motivation of new acceptors" was initiated (Parsons, 1984:6). Together with the integration of family planning services into maternal and child health programs, these strategies proved effective in meeting or exceeding annual targets.

The village contraceptive distribution center (VCDC), which was the next innovation, was aimed at cutting travel time to clinics, making it easier for new acceptors to continue using services. In Java, houses were mapped for potential contraceptors, while in Central and East Java some households were marked with emblems indicating the presence of married couples and their potential for, or use of family planning methods (Parsons, 1984). Others in the community were thus made readily aware of the contraceptive decisions taking place within individual homes. Once a number of households indicated that a particular method had been accepted for use, any stigma previously attached to acceptance of that method was greatly reduced. In fact, it has been suggested that in some cases the stigma instead became associated with the failure to use contraception.

Both the community and the government have played important roles in the program effort. Resources such as "livestock cooperatives, loan cooperatives, irrigation schemes, as well as income generating schemes for acceptors," have been provided by the government as rewards and incentives to villages with good family planning records (Parsons, 1984:14). Among civil servants, current policies limit financial support to three children. These policies are expected to evolve further to a point at which couples will have to consider carefully the impact of their family planning decisions upon the other social services they will receive and the taxes they will pay (Suparlan and Sigit, 1980). One central objective is that a "perceptual link will be created in the minds of individuals that fertility limitation does contribute directly to a higher standard of living for the individual, the family and the community" (Parsons, 1984:14). Planners are thus hoping that members of the community will exert increasing pressure on their neighbors in order to raise village success rates.

Attention has also focused on constraints faced by different religious groups, particularly those in the Moslem community, that limit their participation in the family planning program. In order to increase contraceptive acceptance among Moslems, the BKKBN has stepped up contacts at the village level with "religious leaders, schools (pesantren), and youth and women's organizations; ... [has included] Moslem scholars (ulama) on mobile medical team visits and family planning promotional drives (safari); and [has increased] cooperation with major Moslem assemblies and councils" (Lerman et al., 1989: 35). Available data suggest that all of these efforts have met with success.

As the data in Table 3.5 indicate, significant declines in fertility have already occurred throughout Java, and in Indonesia as a whole. Further declines are expected in the future, as it is generally the women from the younger cohorts who are now limiting their fertility. Since younger and older women have been responding differently to different motivating factors, it is certainly plausible that a generational component might predict acceleration in fertility decreases still ahead. Hull and Hull (1984) contend that the declines that have been observed to date have been due largely to changes in two of the proximate determinants of overall fertility: the proportions married, and the impact of contraceptive use upon the level of fertility within marriage.

The government's family planning program has clearly been instrumental in bringing about increases in the use of birth control;

> the state ideology, in both its early nationalist vigour and its recent formalized indoctrination, has emphasized the complementary themes of individual duty to work for national welfare and

individual rights to personal fulfillment, both of which have been
linked to the practice of birth control through the concept of the
'small, happy, prosperous family', which is the explicit goal of the
family planning program (Hull and Hull, 1984:101).

Estimates of contraceptive prevalence across Indonesia and within specific
regions for 1984, are presented in Table 3.6. To a certain extent the
statistics mirror the total fertility rates presented in Table 3.5. Reported
contraceptive prevalence rates are highest in Yogyakarta, while the total
fertility rate is the lowest there. East Java follows closely on both
indicators. Excluding Jakarta, Central Java has the third highest
contraceptive prevalence rate and the third lowest total fertility rate.
Western Java lags behind on both variables.

National statistics indicate that the success of programs in the rural
portions of the country matches that of programs in the urban centers.
Current use rates as of the 1980 Census varied little between urban and
rural areas, as 26.2 percent of urban residents and roughly 27 percent of
rural residents were currently using a method of birth control at the time of
that enumeration.

As has been mentioned, discussions about the use of family planning
methods are not uncommon in Javanese households. This research
examines the potential effects of residential mobility and the amount of
contact that is maintained with parents after marriage, upon the amount of
input women have into contraceptive decisions, and upon whether or not
actual use is ever made of family planning services. It is expected that
diminished contact with parents on both sides of the family should
precipitate increases in decision-making power within the family for the
wife. Women who are able to exercise more control over household
decisions should in turn be more likely to use contraception, and to have
lower overall fertility than should those with little to say in determining
such matters.

SUMMARY

In summary, women contribute a substantial amount to the family
economy in Indonesia. Although the returns to their labor are generally
low, they are frequently active in the labor force. The more needy the
family, the more likely women are to seek outside employment, and to work
protracted hours. When the combination of directly and indirectly
productive activities is considered, women work roughly 2.4 more hours per
day than do their male counterparts. Since men usually spend more hours
in directly productive work than do their wives, the difference is due largely
to varying inputs into domestic activities. It is interesting to note, however,
that both men and women look after their children when the latter are very
young.

For this and other reasons, women are thought to enjoy relatively high status within Indonesian households. Decisions are often made jointly, particularly among more educated and wealthy couples, and women are especially likely to play an active role in decisions about household finances. As a result, some writers have argued that any problems pertaining to the status of women in rural Java tend to be the result of the local economic environment rather than direct discrimination (Mangkuprawira, 1981).

In the chapters that follow, an attempt will be made to estimate how much control women in Central Java actually have over household decisions, and to note how different factors affect the decision-making dynamics within the household. Vreede-de Stuers (1960:160) claims that the "old attitude of women, based on their dependence on protection by men... is now being replaced by a feeling of selfconfidence which arises from the fact that the modern woman... knows how to make herself useful to her home." Among the goals of this research is to determine whether the traditional props for high fertility are overridden by this and other elements of social change, in combination with the government's efforts to raise contraceptive use and lower total fertility.

NOTES

1. Data on Java are combined with those in Madura.

2. Rural unemployment is also higher among women than it is among men (11 and 7 percent respectively).

3. In other words, women have a great deal to say about financial matters and may be allowed to be chief legal heir.

4. Islamic law.

5. According to this view, the effects of modernization were not those commonly expected to transpire; i.e., not only did modernization fail to bring about improvements in the status of women, but it had the opposite effect.

6. These customs are all heavily biased in favor of the male.

7. Forced marriages are still allowed under *adat*, but it is now also acceptable for young couples to elope and to be reconciled with their parents upon their return.

8. "These advantages" are thought to refer to contact with western civilization.

9. This argument is contradicted by the findings of Mangkuprawira (1981) who contends that in rural areas, where most of the jobs available to women involve unskilled labor positions, increases in eduction do not appear to improve female labor force participation. Instead, the percentage of women employed in the wage economy has been found to be inversely correlated with the levels of schooling completed.

10. The research by Nag et al. is more recent than that of Koentjaraningrat and so is more likely to reflect the current situation among Indonesian families.

4

The Sample, Methods, and Variable Definitions

The data utilized in this research were obtained during a 1985 survey of households in rural Central Java. The survey was conducted in conjunction with LEKNAS/LIPI in Indonesia. Funding was provided by a grant from the Ford Foundation to Brown University for the study of comparative urbanization. Living expenses were covered in part by a traineeship from the National Institutes of Health.

THE SELECTION OF THE SAMPLE

The district within which the sample was drawn was selected because it is characterized by a system of predominantly wet rice agricultural production, and because it is not isolated geographically.[1] Both of these qualities were necessary for the purposes of the other researchers involved in the survey, but the lack of geographical isolation was also important for this investigation. Villages with greater access to urban centers were expected to experience higher rates of mobility to and from those centers (Shaw, 1975), and thus to have greater exposure to more "modern" values and attitudes, than were villages not having similar access. Such values and attitudes include those pertaining to the roles and statuses of women, contraception, family size preferences, and views about the extent to which marriages should be arranged.

The district *(kabupaten)* selected on the basis of these criteria was Sukoharjo. (See Figure 4.1). Central Java is comprised of 29 such *kabupaten,* and Sukoharjo appeared to best address the needs of the project organizers. For the purposes of this research it was an appropriate choice given its proximity to the urban center, Solo.[2] In order to meet the needs of the other researchers, the villages chosen had to be classified as rural and had to be primarily rice-growing locales. They were selected to minimize variation on the predominant type of agriculture, access to urban facilities, and thus mobility, but they were also supposed to enhance variability on

54

FIGURE 4.1: MAP OF JAVA SHOWING LOCATION OF PROVINCES AND KABUPATEN SUKOHARJO

the level of commercialization within the agricultural system.

Given these restrictions, 83 out of the 167 villages in Kabupaten Sukoharjo were found to be appropriate for the larger field project. Twenty-four were eliminated because they were classified as urban,[3] while many of the villages in the southern and western sections of the *kabupaten* were eliminated because their mountainous terrain largely precluded wet rice *(sawah)* production. Given the constraints of the other researchers, the villages that were selected tended to cluster in the northern and central portions of the district. All of the potentially suitable villages were then ranked "according to a measure of agricultural commercialization and one village from each quartile of the ranking was randomly selected" (Guest, 1987:56).

The four villages eventually chosen are from three different sub-districts (or *kecamatan)* within Sukoharjo as a whole. (See Figure 4.2, p. 66). Two of the villages, Mandan and Kenep, are contained within Kecamatan Sukoharjo. Both are located southwest of the district capital, which is also called Sukoharjo.[4] Mandan is roughly two kilometers away from that center, and Kenep is about seven kilometers away. Although not in Kecamatan Sukoharjo, the third village, Jombor, is directly adjacent to the district capital. It lies just north of Sukoharjo and is contained within Kecamatan Bendosari. Finally, Wonorejo is in Kecamatan Polokarto, and is located roughly 13 kilometers northeast of the capital of Sukoharjo.

Once the villages were chosen, 160 households were selected within each one. Although the largest possible sample size was the goal, budgetary constraints eventually determined the target number of households.

A household was defined as "a group of persons who eat and cook together, or [who] had done so within the last five years... [The] definition was based on previous research and is considered to define an economic unit in Javanese society" (Guest, 1987: 84). Since the village with the fewest households had 696 (Kenep), while that with the most had 788 (Mandan), the number of households varied little between villages. As a consequence, it was not necessary to weight the sample. The target population included all households in the four villages.

Village registers were used to select the households. These registers are made up of lists of all household members by age, sex, and religion. Less complete information is available on the primary occupations and educational attainment levels of household members, and on the consumer goods they own. The lists are utilized for Census enumerations, village statistical reports, and the issuance of identification cards, and so are generally assumed to be maintained with reasonable accuracy. While they

TABLE 4.1:   SELECTED VILLAGE CHARACTERISTICS

	Jombor	Kenep	Mandan	Wonorejo
Total population	3,824	3,165	4,028	3,631
Total land area (km2)	2.36	2.82	3.18	2.26
Population density	1,620	1,122	1,238	1,607

have been utilized as sampling frames in other studies on Indonesia, problems have at times arisen from their use; e.g., lists have been out of date or incomplete. In spite of the limitations, Hugo (1982) has argued that these problems are apt to be less severe in Java than elsewhere in Indonesia, and that village registers in that province are probably suitable for use as sampling frames as long as appropriate precautions are taken.

Village registers were available for all four of the villages selected for this research, but they varied in level of completeness and method of upkeep. In Jombor and Mandan, the registers were maintained by the head of each neighborhood *(ketua rukun tetangga* (R.T.)), or administrative unit. Each R.T. averages around 30 households. Officials from both villages claimed that their registers were regularly updated, and both sets of listings were approximately one year old. It was discovered, however, that three of the R.T.s in Mandan had no registers, and the appropriate lists had to be constructed in order for those neighborhoods to be included in the sampling frame.

In Kenep separate registers were not kept for each R.T. Instead there were three registers, each covering a number of the neighborhoods. Again, all three were supposed to be updated on a regular basis, yet one R.T. was missing from the listings. The official in charge of that register (the *kebayan*, or link between the top village office and the neighborhood), explained that R.T. was too far away to attain the appropriate information. As a result, a special register also had to be constructed for that neighborhood. Finally, in Wonorejo there was only one register and it had not been updated since the 1980 Census.

A preliminary survey was conducted in each neighborhood in all four villages in order to 1) check the accuracy of these registers, 2) obtain information about household mobility (to further update the registers), 3) gather insights into local household structures, and 4) accustom people to the idea of the upcoming formal survey.

The data gathered during the informal preliminary survey were then compared with those available through the household registers. In Jombor, Kenep, and Mandan the results indicated that the registers were of sufficiently high quality to allow them to be used in the sampling frame. In Wonorejo, however, the register was badly out of date and highly inaccurate. As a result, it was disqualified from the sampling frame and a household register maintained by officials in charge of family planning was tested. The family planning roster contained data on the name, sex, age, and often the family planning status of household members. It was found to be quite accurate, and so was also approved for the sampling frame.

Once the preliminary sampling frame was established, it was updated by the heads of each neighborhood. Households that had dissolved because of the death or out-migration of its members were eliminated from the sampling frame, and those newly created through in-migration or other relocation were added. A preliminary sample of 160 households was then drawn from each of the updated registers.

> The registers were arranged by R.T. so there existed an internal stratification by geographic area within the village. The sampling method used was systematic sampling with a random start. After the initial sample selection, a further systematic sample of 10 households from the original survey was undertaken. These 10 households were to serve as replacement if, for any reason, it was not possible to obtain interview households from the sample (Guest, 1987:91).

Unfortunately, however, given the length of the questionnaire administered to the household heads, and given limited time and financial resources, it soon became apparent that completion of the survey under existing conditions would be unlikely. It was therefore necessary to reduce the sample to 130 households per village, and to do so by restricting the sample to households in which the household head was aged 60 or less. This decision was made for several reasons, (e.g., older respondents are often more difficult to interview than younger individuals), but was particularly important for this research. Since the aim of this investigation was to interview women who were still in or close to their childbearing years, most women married to men well over 60 years of age would eventually have been excluded from the reduced sample utilized in this study. The decision to restrict the sample to households headed by younger individuals thus ensured that the specific sub-sample utilized for this research would not be radically reduced.

In cases in which the age restriction lowered the village samples below the targeted 130 households, substitutes from the replacement sample were used. If all replacements were included and the target still fell short of the 130 households needed per village, the original households were replaced by the households closest to them. When the final sample for the complete field project was drawn, it was viewed as a representative sample of households headed by males aged 60 or less. Female headed households are probably under-represented, however.[5]

Eventually the members of 522 households were interviewed. There was only one household refusal. Of the 1348 individuals who were members of the households selected, however, 25 were sick or could not be located. As a result, information on them as well as on the 240 household members who lived outside the village, was obtained from other members of the household. In this research, the unit of analysis is the individual woman. The sample has been limited to all currently married women aged 50 or less, along with their husbands in cases in which interview data are available on them. As a result, 453 women and approximately 400 husbands comprise the final sample.

The basic age and sex distribution of the sample utilized in this research (minus the men over age 50) is presented by village in Table 4.2. As would be anticipated, the women tend to be younger as a group than do the men, but there is nothing otherwise striking about this distribution. No major differences are observed between villages, and no highly unusual patterns occur within any of the groups within villages.

THE INTERVIEWING

The interviewers recruited to conduct the survey were all university students from the Universitas Sebelas Maret in Solo, the urban center adjacent to the *kabupaten* (Sukoharjo) in which the survey was to take place. Twelve men and twelve women were hired in all. All had rural backgrounds and spoke Javanese. Two days were spent at the university for interviewer training, most of which involved going over the questionnaire. Upon completion of the training session, the interviewers moved to households in the villages selected by village officials.

The interviewers operated in teams. One male and one female went to each of the sampled households. The information on the household schedule was obtained first. During that section of the interview it was often helpful to have several household members present to fill in gaps in the primary respondent's answers. Given the focus of the this research, however, it was imperative that both male and female respondents answer frankly and freely. As a consequence, after the household schedule had been completed, interviewers were instructed to conduct interviews of individuals separately. The male interviewers were assigned to interview male household members, and the female interviewers were assigned to interview the women.

TABLE 4.2: AGE-SEX DISTRIBUTION OF THE SAMPLE BY
VILLAGE

Sex:	Jombor M	F	Kenep M	F	Mandan M	F	Wonorejo M	F
Age								
< 20	0.0	1.6	1.0	1.8	0.0	1.0	0.0	1.7
20-24	6.5	17.1	4.1	14.1	1.2	13.6	4.3	6.9
25-29	18.5	21.1	13.4	23.4	17.7	23.3	16.1	22.4
30-34	15.2	13.0	24.7	14.4	21.5	10.7	24.7	23.3
35-39	15.2	14.6	12.3	15.3	13.9	15.5	21.5	13.8
40-44	17.4	14.6	13.4	12.6	15.1	14.6	12.9	11.2
45-50	27.2	17.9	30.9	18.0	30.4	21.4	20.4	20.7
Total %	100.0	100.0	100.0	100.0	100.0	100.0	100.0	100.0
Number	92	123	97	111	79	103	93	116

Considerable care was taken to interview husbands and wives both separately and simultaneously to avoid contamination of the results. In some cases, however, that was not possible given the work obligations of the respondents. In Mandan, for example, it was harvest time for many households, and family members took turns coming in from the fields to be interviewed. Although this system did not allow for simultaneous interviews, it did ensure that spouses would be interviewed separately. When it was not possible to conduct the interviews simultaneously, they were almost always completed within a few hours of one another, minimizing the amount of time in which discussion between the two spouses could have taken place between interviews.

The separation of spouses was particularly important for questions involving the relative power of individuals in making major household decisions. Those questions are central to the analysis of the inter-generational dynamics involved in the marriage decision, as well as to the estimation of women's intra-household status; both are among the most complex concepts to be analyzed in this research.

VARIABLE DEFINITIONS AND ANALYSIS

The first dependent variable measures the amount of input the respondent felt she/he had into the decision that he/she should marry his/her current spouse. This variable is categorized one through five, with a five indicating that the respondent (and in most cases the spouse) had complete control over the decision to marry, a four indicating that the decision was primarily theirs although others had some input, a three indicating that they shared equally with others in making the decision, a two indicating that the decision was largely made by others, but that they were allowed some input, and a one indicating that the respondent had no control at all over the marriage decision. Respondents were asked to decide which category best fit their recollection of the marriage decision, but their answers are meant to be viewed as falling somewhere along a continuum of relative power. The median response offered by women to this question is 4.0, and the skewness of the distribution is minimal (.049).

In cases in which the couple was not solely responsible for the marriage decision it is certainly possible that women and men were allowed different amounts of input into the decision, i.e., that they did not act as equal partners or as a unit in the process. Although this variable was designed to measure the extent to which parents and other family members controlled the marriage decision, it is thus limited in that it fails to capture explicitly the different levels of input enjoyed by the brides and the grooms themselves. As the information provided in Chapter 5 will demonstrate, however, some differences in their perceptions of power may nonetheless be analyzed.

The independent variables introduced into each set of equations aimed at estimating this dependent variable are, for the most part, straightforward. Union order is a simple dichotomous variable, with a zero indicating that the respondent was in his/her first marriage at the time of the survey, and a one indicating a higher-order union. Variables measuring the educational attainment levels of the fathers of the respondents are categorized one through five, with a one indicating no formal schooling and a five indicating completion of at least some college-level education. These values are then multiplied by three to approximate the average number of years of schooling attained by the fathers at each level of education, and to make the coefficients generated more compatible with those measuring the schooling levels of the respondents themselves. Respondents' educational attainment levels are measured by the total number of years of formal schooling each completed.

As is true of the dependent decision-making variable, the categories of these independent variables are described only in order to give the reader an understanding of the organization of the data. The divisions of the education variables, like those that comprise the decision-making variables and many of the others presented in this discussion, are meant to be viewed as part of a continuum, and not as discrete groups.

The variable measuring residence prior to marriage is divided into four categories. A four indicates residence in Jakarta, a three indicates other metropolitan residence (one million plus residents), a two represents life in another large urban area (cities of 250,000 to 999,999 residents), and a one indicates residence in a smaller urban or rural setting. It would have been preferable to have separate information on small urban versus rural locales, and in fact, the questionnaire was designed to allow for this distinction. Unfortunately, however, the data were collapsed into the groupings listed above during the coding process.

Age at marriage (for the current union), measured in years, is included as a control in several of the equations because younger grooms, and especially younger brides, are considered to be more malleable than are more mature adults (Caldwell et al., 1983). The age at which individuals marry has also been found to increase with rising educational levels, modernization, and urbanization (Smith, 1980; Smith and Karim, 1980). The duration of the couple's marriage is included as an indicator of marriage cohort. Considerable emphasis has been placed on the element of time in studies of family change, and the inclusion of the duration of marriage variable is appropriate to measure its effects. Construction of this variable is also straightforward; it measures the number of years the respondent has been married to his/her current spouse.

Measurement of Female Status

Chapter 6 focuses on the determinants of the woman's status within the household once she is married. In the analysis in that chapter, the variable measuring input into the marriage decision is used as a predictor of the new dependent variables measuring intra-household status.

As has been mentioned, the concept of the status of women has been defined in a number of different ways. One relatively comprehensive, but broad definition suggests that status includes the elements of "the degree of women's access to (and control over) material resources (including food, income, land, and other forms of wealth) and to social resources (including knowledge, power, and prestige)..." (Dixon, 1978:6). Safilios-Rothschild (1982) has further demonstrated the complexity of this concept by distinguishing between different types of status, such as gender and SES, emphasizing the importance of their interrelationships and separating status on the interpersonal level, called "power," from that on a broader scale.

Since this research is primarily concerned with status (or power) within the family, concepts related to this form of status will be addressed first. These include among others: the "ability to control decisions about... productive and economic activities, including the freedom of movement and control over the resulting wages or income" (Safilios-Rothschild, 1982:128), the power to direct the services of others who aid or fill in for the woman in her domestic responsibilities, the ability to control the composition of the household, the amount of leisure time the wife has compared to her husband, and the amount of input she has in major decisions such as family size (including whether or not, and if so, when to have a child), migration, and large purchases (Safilios-Rothschild, 1982).

Of these components of status, the power to have an input in major decisions is of primary importance to this research. Of the several elements initially considered,[6] questions relating to the decision-making process were found to be the easiest to convey to the respondents. As a consequence, the status of women within the family was indexed on the basis of their decision-making power in several central aspects of their lives. As was true of the marriage decision questions, the respondent was asked for each decision whether 1) she alone made the decision (i.e., she had complete control), 2) she had primary control of the decision, but others were allowed some input, 3) she shared about equally with others in making the decision, 4) the decision was primarily made by others, but she was allowed some input, or 5) the decision was made entirely by other individuals, and she was allowed no input whatsoever. Husbands were also asked how much control they had over important household decisions, and the questions addressed to them followed the same format.

All together five dependent variables are analyzed in Chapter 6. Four measure the status of women as perceived by the women themselves, and a fifth measures their husbands' views of their input into the decision-making process. Of the variables that pertain to the female respondents, one measures women's inputs into decisions regarding resource control, one measures their control over fertility decisions, one measures decisions regarding ever-use of contraception, and one is a composite indicator. The first of these four, the resource control variable, measures the amount of control women who earn a cash income feel they have over decisions regarding how that income is utilized. The second measures how the decision to stop childbearing was made, for women who claim they plan to have no further children. The third measures how ever-users of birth control decided to adopt contraception for the first time, and for the fourth variable, an average and standardized score of the woman's power as measured by the other three variables was calculated. Finally, the fifth variable is a composite measure for the husband's score based on the same three indicators.[7]

It might be expected that once a couple is married, the decisions made within the household should primarily involve the two spouses, and indeed that is often the case. On the other hand, parents in Indonesia frequently maintain an active interest in the lives of their adult children, and continue to take part in intra-household decision-making after the couple has married.

Predictors of Intra-Household Status

Variables measuring one of the predictors expected to be central to the estimation of intra-familial decision-making power, the mobility of the couple following their marriage, are operationalized into four categories. In every case but one, a move is said to occur if the individual(s) in question changed residence within four years following the marriage, as four years is the normative period of time in which a post-marriage inter-household (and possibly inter-village) move generally takes place in rural Indonesia (Koentjaraningrat, 1967). The five mobility categories created include 1) that in which neither spouse moved, 2) that in which only the wife relocated, 3) that in which only her husband moved, 4) that in which both moved within four years of marriage, and 5) that in which they both moved, but only after four years. The category in which both moved within four years of marriage is used as the reference category because it is expected to be the category yielding the greatest intra-familial power for the woman.[8]

The other mobility variable measures moves between villages and the timing of those relocations. If the woman migrated to a new village within four years of her marriage, she is represented in one dummy category. If she completed an inter-village move, but not until she had been married for four or more years, she is in another, and if she did not participate in any move beyond the borders of her village since her marriage, she is in the reference group. These variables are included to determine whether longer distance moves are disruptive to women, or whether they help them gain independence from outside interference in the decision-making process. The variable is also conceptualized in this way to determine whether or not the timing of such moves affects women's intra-household status.

To further examine the importance of parental inputs into familial decisions, a variable that measures the amount of contact between the respondent and his or her parents is introduced. Respondents were asked how often on average they visited with each parent. If they were living with either or both parents, they obviously reported frequent interactions with them. For each parent the respondent was asked whether interactions occurred on average: more than once a week, about once a week, two or three times a month, roughly once a month, at least once a year but not every month, or less than once a year.[9]

The actual parental contact variable was then constructed as follows. Respondents who had frequent contact (at least once a week) with either or both of their own parents were listed as having frequent parental contact, and those who saw neither of their parents as often as once a week were listed as not having frequent contact. Dummy variables were constructed such that 1) one group was composed of couples among whom only the wife had frequent contact with her parents, 2) another contained only those in which the husband had frequent contact with his parents, 3) a third contained couples in which both spouses frequently saw their parents, and 4) the fourth group was composed of couples among whom neither spouse had frequent contact with her/his parents. The latter group was used as the reference category.

These variables can only approximate the amount of contact that took place between the respondents and their parents at the time of the contraception and fertility decisions because the contact is measured at the time of the survey, not at the time of the decision. Since some parents would have died between the time of the decision and the time of the survey, and other sets of parents and children would have altered their visitation patterns, there are limitations associated with these variables. However, these limitations are expected to be less restrictive than might be expected. For instance, the fertility decision involves only women who had completed their childbearing before they were interviewed. Because the upper age limit on the sample is 50, most who had discontinued childbearing would not have done so long prior to the survey. For the question involving control of resources, the causal order is not an issue, since both variables were measured at the time of the survey. The only set of equations for which the temporal sequence is of somewhat greater concern is that involving the ever-use of contraception.

In many of the equations the respondent's input into the marriage decision is introduced as an independent variable. Its construction has already been described. Income variables are also straightforward. Log transformations of the wife's earnings tended to improve the linearity of the relationship between her income and the dependent variable, while similar transformations of her husband's earnings were generally not helpful.[10] The natural log value of the wife's earnings in *rupiahs* (plus one to accommodate the log transformation in cases in which her earnings equalled zero (25 percent of the cases)) thus forms the independent variable for her income, and a similar transformation was made for her husband's income where appropriate. Otherwise, the variable measuring the husband's income is simply the number of *rupiahs* he earned per year, divided by 1000.

Urban residence was not found to be significant in the estimation of women's status and so was dropped from the analysis.

Contraception and Fertility

In the final analysis chapter, the dependent variables are the ever-use or non-use of contraception, and the number of children ever born to the respondent at the time of the survey. In the case of the former, the dependent variable is dichotomous, with a one indicating that the couple had used contraceptives during this marital union, and a zero indicating that no such use had occurred. The second variable is simply the total number of children the woman had ever borne.

In that chapter, the woman's decision-making power within the family is introduced as an independent predictor of both contraceptive use and fertility. However, the resource control variable is utilized as the sole predictor of women's status in lieu of the composite measure, because the other components of status are highly related to the dependent variable measuring contraceptive use. Since only women who had used contraception were asked questions pertaining to contraceptive decision-making, all those who were never-users were coded zero on that variable. Further, the women in this sample who had used contraception appear to have done so primarily for child stopping, rather than spacing purposes. As a consequence, a large proportion of women who were ever-users of contraception have non-zero scores on both decision-making variables, while many non-users do not have scores (other than zero) for the variable measuring input into contraception decisions, and relatively few have non-zero scores for the variable measuring power in the childbearing decision. Because 75 percent of the women in the sample earned a cash income in the year preceding the survey, the resource control variable was best suited for this portion of the analysis. Although the constraints against using the composite indicator were less severe in examining actual fertility, the same procedure was followed for the parity estimations.

The mobility variables utilized in the contraception equations are similar to those described above, but the timing of the move is disregarded. Whether the wife or the husband moved alone, they moved together, or neither one moved, is the central issue. These variables are examined along with the variables measuring the educational attainment of each spouse, the woman's income (logged), and the length of time the couple had spent in the current union. Because a slight curvilinear association between contraception and marital duration was observed in preliminary bivariate analyses, the duration variable was categorized into three dummies. The first includes those who had been married for fifteen years or less, the second is made up of those married 16 to 25 years, and the third includes those married for 26 years or more. The size of the community in which the woman lived prior to marriage (as defined earlier) was found to have a significant bivariate association with the dependent variable and so has also been included in this part of the analysis.

The only additional variables utilized in Chapter 7 include one that measures the desire for additional children, and one measuring the frequency with which discussions about contraception had taken place between the husband and the wife. The former is a simple dichotomy, with a one indicating that the wife intended to have additional children (27.7 percent of the sample), and a zero indicating that she did not (72.3 percent of the sample). For the variable measuring the amount of discussion that had taken place between the wife and her husband on the subject of contraception, a zero indicated that no discussion had taken place, a one that such discussions had occurred only very rarely, a two indicated that they had taken place somewhat more often, a three that they happened quite often, and a four indicated that they had occurred very often. The research supervisors advised against attempting to get greater detail on this variable.

Because the dependent variable is dichotomous, all independent variables were regressed on the dependent variable in a logistic regression using the program, LIMDEP.

For the final set of equations, those estimating the determinants of children ever born to the women in this sample, the only independent

variable not already defined is one that measures the number of children
the wife believed to be ideal. The distribution on that variable is presented
in Chapter 7 and the variable is self-explanatory. Whether or not the
couple had ever used contraception is included in the second of the two
equations in the set, and is categorized as described above. In the final set
of equations standard ordinary least squares regression techniques are
utilized.

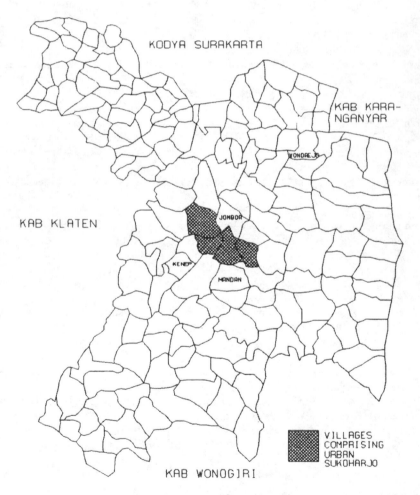

FIGURE 4.2:   LOCATION OF URBAN SUKOHARJO AND SAMPLE VILLAGES

NOTES

1. For more detailed information about the sample selection, see Guest (1987).

2. Solo's population in 1980 was 469,532, making that city the second most populous in the province of Central Java (Indonesia, Biro Statistik, 1983).

3. Sixteen of these comprised or abutted the Solo-Kartusoro urban center, and four formed portions of the district capital of Sukoharjo.

4. The population of Sukoharjo in 1980 was listed as 7992 (Indonesia, Biro Pusat Statistik, 1980), but the built-up area around Sukoharjo is actually comprised of four villages. For practical purposes, the total population of the urban area was 24,006.

5. One household also had to be dropped from the sample because of the mental handicaps of its members.

6. For example, although the differences in the amounts of leisure time available to husband and wife has been argued to be quite large in Java, (with the man reportedly working approximately two and a half fewer hours per day than does his spouse (Birdsall and McGreevey, 1983)), leisure time is particularly difficult to estimate as Javanese do not have a clear conception of time, and the distinction between leisure and work activities is often vague.

7. Both composite indicators have been standardized by subtracting the mean from each value on the three separate components, and then dividing by the standard deviation.

8. Pre-marital cohabitation is virtually unheard of in rural Javanese populations.

9. Parents who were no longer living fell into the last category. They were not excluded from the analysis, but rather viewed as an extreme end of the continuum. Since older respondents were apt to be those with deceased parents, the exclusion of each case of a non-living parent would have meant lost information on an important category of respondents, and would have further reduced the number of cases.

10. Even after the log transformation, husbands' income exhibited no significant bivariate relationship to decision-making power.

5

Intergenerational Dynamics
in the Marriage Decision

In more developed societies, complete parental control over the marriage decision (and other types of decisions as well) began to erode some time ago. Explanations differ as to which factors played the greatest part in bringing about the transfer of power within the western family (Stone, 1977; Thadani, 1978), and varying rationales for what is seen as the parallel transition in today's developing countries are now also being posited. Goode (1963) has argued that urbanization and industrialization have been largely responsible for the realignment throughout much of the world. As the possibility for the inheritance of land decreases, the importance of such inheritance as a means by which parents control children declines as well. Instead, as educational opportunities grow, parents try to ensure that all children attain some schooling. In some cases, education then becomes a form of dower or dowry. Once the process of differentiation begins to take hold, with educational and productive activities increasingly taking place outside the home (Smelser, 1968), the ability of parents to control the future economic security of their children declines, as does their bargaining power.

With this type of family transformation well underway in the more developed nations, the diffusion of relevant western values and attitudes has been seen as a major determinant of family evolution in less developed regions (Caldwell, 1976). According to Smith (1980), education and urbanization (both of which facilitate the process of diffusion), along with growth in non-agricultural employment opportunities, play a vital role in the process in Asia. Mass education is seen as important because it provides a view of the family that is based on a western model, either because the textbooks are acquired directly from a western producer, or because they are designed to emulate western texts (Caldwell, 1976). Again, because development transfers usually accrue first to the more modern urban sectors in developing countries (Gugler, 1982; Arndt, 1983), exposure to imported western values tends to be more pronounced in urban centers than in outlying areas. Both higher education and residence in an urban community prior to marriage are therefore thought to play primary roles in decreasing the relative inputs of parents compared to children in making the final marriage decision.

Also of importance is the age at which the respondent marries. Not only is there a general tendency for the average age at marriage to increase with rising educational levels and urbanization (Smith, 1980; Smith and Karim, 1980), but it is fairly clear that younger grooms, and especially younger brides, are more easily controlled by older family members than are more mature adults (Caldwell et al., 1983). If individuals marry when they are still little more than children, the decision will be implemented almost exclusively by their elders. As the age at marriage increases, parental control should diminish. Further, because it is frequently the custom for men to marry women younger than themselves (Casterline et al., 1986), and because males tend to be more highly educated than females (The World Bank, 1984), it should also follow that men will report having had more input into the marriage decision than will their wives.

It is reasonable to expect, however, that gender differences in perceptions of power will often remain after both education and age at marriage are controlled. This should be true to varying degrees among the marriage cohorts covered in this analysis of rural Java. Among the earlier cohorts, arranged marriages were unquestionably the norm; a son or daughter relinquished control of the marriage decision to his parents as "a symbol of his psychological dependency on them, of his acceptance of his future responsibilities toward them in their old age, and of his lesser status in regard to them" (Geertz, 1961:56). Compared to sons, however, daughters had even less to say about whom they would marry. According to Geertz (1961:56) "parents usually wait until their son feels himself ready for marriage and comes to them for help. They often allow him to indicate the girl he wants or to veto their suggestions." While many believe that women enjoy a high level of autonomy within the family in Indonesia today, this is not without exception, particularly among lower social classes (Mangkuprawira, 1981; Hull, 1976), and does not necessarily translate from equal status prior to marriage.

As has been discussed, parents on both sides of the family continue to take part to varying degrees in the process of mate selection, particularly for a first marriage, with the chosen spouse being one who is expected to strengthen the existing family. On the other hand, it has become increasingly common for the preferences of both the bride and groom to be taken into consideration in the selection process. When their preferences are disregarded, or when the match is unsuccessful for other reasons, it has also become acceptable for individuals to defer to their parents and marry a designated spouse, only to divorce and remarry the next time to someone more of their own choosing (Ihromi et al., 1973).[1] Since sons and daughters have begun to play an expanded role in the mate selection process, unions have become seemingly more stable and divorces less prevalent (Hugo et al., 1987).

Given the information presented thus far, the following relationships are hypothesized to hold:

(5.1) Individuals with more education will have had more input into decisions affecting their own marriages than will those with less education.

(5.2) Individuals with more educated parents will have had more input into decisions affecting their own marriages than will those with less educated parents.

(5.3) Individuals who lived in a large urban area prior to marriage will have had more input into decisions affecting their own marriages than will those who lived in small urban or rural areas.

(5.4) Respondents who were married recently will have had more input into decisions affecting their marriages than will those wed longer ago.

(5.5) Those who married at older ages will have had more input into the marriage decision than will those who married at younger ages.

(5.6) Men will report having had more input into the marriage decision than will their spouses.

(5.7) Those currently in second or higher order marriages will have had more input into the marriage decisions involving the current union than will those still in their first marriages.

SPOUSAL PERCEPTIONS OF POWER IN THE MARRIAGE DECISION

Frequencies pertaining to both male and female respondents' perceptions of their inputs into decisions regarding spousal selections are presented in Table 5.1. In general, the spread across categories of the dependent variable is fairly even, especially among women. Frequencies of male and female responses for each level of input are also quite similar in categories two through four, in which the couple shares control over the marriage decision to varying degrees with other family members.

Where men and women do differ, however, is in the extreme categories. Men are considerably more likely to feel that they and their spouses had total control over the marriage decision than are women. And men are much less likely to feel that they had no input into the decision than are their wives. While 20.3 percent of the women feel that they had no control over the selection of their spouses, only 10.9 percent of the men surveyed fall into that category. Conversely, whereas 23.6 percent of the husbands feel that the marriage decision was completely in the hands of the couple, only 16.8 percent of the wives felt no outside pressure in making the decision to marry.

This suggests that, at least among certain segments of this sample, males did have more to say in choosing their spouses than did females. As Geertz (1961) indicated, among more traditional couples for whom marriages are arranged, males appear to have been completely left out of the decision far less often than females. Similarly, among couples at the opposite end of the scale, those who exercise considerable freedom in choosing a spouse, men also appear to operate under fewer familial constraints than do women.

Crosstabulated responses of husbands and wives are presented in Table 5.2. They indicate that a slight majority of husbands and wives actually agree precisely as to the amount of input they had in the decision making process; just over half of the pairs (52.6 percent) fall somewhere on the diagonal. For those among whom some disagreement does exist, however, males generally report fewer parental constraints than do females. Almost twice as many paired respondents fall above the diagonal as fall below it, again demonstrating that men at least perceive themselves to have had more input into the marriage decision than do women. Couples whose perceptions of the decision-making process are radically different are relatively few.

TABLE 5.1:   PERCENT DISTRIBUTION OF PERCEIVED CONTROL
OVER MARRIAGE DECISIONS (WIVES AND THEIR HUSBANDS)

Dependent Variable	Women's Perceptions	Men's Perceptions
No Control	20.3	10.9
Little Control	23.6	25.6
Shared Control	15.7	17.8
Primary Control	23.6	22.1
Complete Control	16.8	23.6
Total percent	100.0	100.0
Total number	394	394

MULTIVARIATE RESULTS

In order to determine which factors most influence the variations in perceptions that do exist, multivariate analyses were conducted for male and female respondents separately; then additional equations were estimated using combined data. Results showing the effects of the central variables upon the women's inputs into the decision-making process are shown in Table 5.3.

In Equation 1, the dependent variable measuring a woman's input into the marriage decision is regressed on variables measuring her education and that of her father, along with her union order and the size of the city/town in which she lived prior to marriage. All results from that equation are significant and in the directions predicted. As educational attainment rises, so does the amount of control women exercise in making the marriage decision. Similarly, as their fathers' schooling increases, so does their input into the process of mate selection. Women in higher-order unions experience greater freedom in choosing their mates than do women in their first marriages, and women residing in larger urban areas prior to marriage have more input into the decision-making process than do women living in smaller urban areas or in rural locales.

TABLE 5.2: HUSBANDS' VERSUS WIVES' INPUT INTO THE MARRIAGE DECISION

Women's Percep- tions	Husbands' Perceptions of their Control Over the Marriage Decision					
	None	Little	Equal	Primary	Complete	Total
None	8.1	5.3	1.8	3.0	2.0	20.3
Little	1.3	13.5	3.8	3.0	2.0	23.6
Equal	-	3.6	7.9	3.6	0.8	15.7
Primary	1.5	2.5	3.0	10.4	6.1	23.6
Complete	-	0.8	1.3	2.0	12.7	16.8
Total %	10.9	25.6	17.8	22.1	23.6	100
Total N	43	101	70	87	93	394

Correlation = .5838; R Square = .341.

TABLE 5.3: FACTORS AFFECTING WOMEN'S PERCEPTIONS OF THEIR DECISION-MAKING POWER IN CHOICE OF SPOUSE (Unstandardized Coefficients)

Independent Variables	Equation 1	2	3
Education:			
Wife's	.069**	.055*	.036
Wife's father's	.078**	.079**	.073**
Wife's union order (0–1st union, 1–higher order)	.452*	.291	.356*
Size of wife's premarital community	.459*	.443*	.426*
Wife's age at marriage	n.a.	.041**	.023
Marital duration	n.a.	n.a.	-.028**
Constant	3.732**	3.192**	3.923**
R Square	.124	.142	.168
Number of respondents	386	386	386

One-tailed tests of significance: * indicates significance at the .05 level; ** indicates significance at the .01 level.

In Equation 2, the dependent variable is again regressed on the education, residence, and union order variables, while a control for the age at which the woman married is added. As expected, the age at marriage variable is found to be of considerable importance; women who marry later have a great deal more to say about whom they will marry than do those wed at earlier ages. Although the education variables and the one measuring size of community prior to marriage remain significant in this estimation, the effects of union order weaken and become non-significant. This is most likely because age at entry into higher-order unions is generally greater than age at first marriage, and much of the effect of the union order variable is absorbed by the one measuring age at marriage.

In the third equation, the variable measuring the duration of the woman's marriage is added to the estimation. This variable was expected to be of considerable importance because it indicates how long ago the marriage decision actually took place. As predicted, those who were married some time ago had considerably less input into the marriage decision than did those who were married more recently. Beta coefficients (not presented) indicate that the marital duration variable is actually the strongest predictor of the woman's input into the mate selection decision of all the variables entered into this equation.[2]

To examine the importance of changes over time in greater detail, the sample was split in half at the median length of marital duration (15 years). This procedure was undertaken to see whether or not the variables of interest were more important for more recently married women or for those married longer ago. Because no specific hypotheses were introduced for this section of the analysis, a two-tailed test of significance was utilized. Results are presented in Table 5.4.

Among the women who had been married for 15 or more years by the time of the survey, the variables measuring the ages at which they married their current husbands, and the sizes of their communities prior to marriage prove to be the factors of central interest. Again, women who got married when they were older had more input into the marriage decision than did those who married early, while women from smaller locales were able to exert less power in making the decision than were those from larger cities. The age at marriage variable is especially important to those married 15 or more years ago, probably because differences between the ages at which women and men got married were larger during that time than has been true more recently.[3]

The importance of the variable measuring the size of the community in which the woman lived prior to her marriage is more pronounced for women married longer ago than it is for those married more recently, probably because 15 years prior to the survey, transportation to and from larger urban centers was much less well developed, and therefore much less utilized than is true today. As a result, exposure to modern values and attitudes was much more likely to occur if the respondent lived in the urban centers than if she lived elsewhere and gained exposure only by travelling into the city at rare intervals. Conversely, recent improvements in roads

TABLE 5.4: FACTORS AFFECTING WOMEN'S PERCEPTIONS OF
THEIR DECISION-MAKING POWER IN CHOICE OF SPOUSE BY
MARITAL DURATION (Unstandardardized Coefficients)

Independent Variables	Married less than 15 years	Married 15 years or more
Education:		
Wife's	.049*	.016
Wife's father's	.206***	.165
Wife's union order (0—1st union, 1—higher-order)	.206	.326
Size of wife's premarital community	.241	.686**
Wife's age at marriage	.018	.032*
Marital duration	-.052**	-.015
Constant	4.865***	5.913***
R Square	.11	.09
Respondents	226	219

Two-tailed tests of significance: * indicates significance at the .10 level; ** indicates significance at the
.05 level; *** indicates significance at the .01 level.

and transportation in general, as well as in employment opportunities for women in the city, are likely to have spurred movement to and from urban areas. The importance of actual residence in the urban center should thus have diminished over time.

Variables that are more salient to recently married women include their educational attainment, the levels of schooling of their fathers, and the length of time spent in the current union. The significance of the marital duration variable only for more recently married women suggests that the most substantial changes in the amount of input they have been allowed into the marriage decision have occurred fairly recently. Variation in the ability or inability of women to play a major role in the marriage decision is therefore likely to be greater among more recent cohorts.

The significance of the variable measuring the education of the women themselves probably reflects changes in the focus of the curriculum over recent years, in combination with vast improvements in female enrollments and continuation rates. The importance of the amount of schooling completed by the fathers probably also reflects, at least to some extent, the changing content of the material presented to them over time.

In summary of this section, the variables of most importance among women married longer ago are the size of their home communities prior to marriage and the ages at which they married their current husbands. Variables measuring the amount of education attained by both the women and their fathers are more important among women married more recently than among those married 15 or more years before the survey, and the same is true of the duration of marriage variable.

Interestingly, many of the variables that are useful in explaining women's perceptions of the marriage decision fail to predict males' responses. The results of the analysis focusing on husbands' perceptions of the decision-making process are presented in Table 5.5. In the first equation, the husband's education, union order, and size of community prior to marriage are all found to have no bearing on his level of control over the marriage decision. Only the educational attainment of the men's fathers is found to be significant. Again, the more schooling the father had completed, the more input the respondent perceived himself to have had in making the decision to marry his current spouse. This effect also holds in the second equation after the variable measuring his age at marriage is introduced. As was true for the women, the husband's age at marriage is a significant predictor of his level of control over the marriage decision, and the coefficient is again positive. Men who married later believe they had more input into the mate selection process than do those who married when they were younger.

In the third equation the marital duration variable is added. The significant effects found in Equations 1 and 2 remain, and marital duration is again found to be a powerful explanatory variable. As was the case in the equations estimating the women's views of the marriage decision, men who were married recently perceive themselves to have had more autonomy in choosing a mate than do those who were married longer ago.

TABLE 5.5: FACTORS AFFECTING HUSBANDS' PERCEPTIONS OF THE MARRIAGE DECISION (Unstandardized Coefficients)

Independent Variables	Equation 1	2	3
Education:			
Husband's	.004	.001	-.016
Husband's father's	.056**	.056**	.055**
Husband's union order (0–1st marriage, 1–higher-order)	.251	.040	.100
Size of husband's community of residence before marriage	.019	-.018	.042
Husband's age at marriage	n.a.	.033**	.025*
Marital duration	n.a.	n.a.	-.025**
Constant	2.831**	2.168**	3.047**
R Square	.034	.053	.078
Number of Respondents	391	391	391

One-tailed tests of significance: * indicates significance at the .05 level; ** indicates significance at the .01 level.

It should be noted that the independent variables included in the analyses do a considerably better job of explaining the variance in the amount of input women claim to have had into the marriage decision (17 percent) than is true for their husbands (8 percent). Initially, it was thought that part of the explanation for this might be that changes over time have been of disproportionate benefit to women in matters concerning the choice of a spouse.

To examine that possiblity, one last set of regression equations was estimated. Male and female responses were combined and the dependent variable, perceptions of input into the marriage decision, was regressed on the independent variables described above. The gender of the respondent was included in the analysis to gauge its importance in the marriage decision-making process. In addition, in the third equation, interaction terms have been included to determine whether the gender of the respondent is a good predictor when entered in combination with either the variable measuring the respondent's education or marital duration. The results are presented in Table 5.6.

In the first equation, the findings are largely as expected. All variables, with the exception of the size of the respondent's community prior to marriage, are significant and in the predicted directions. This includes the variable of central interest in this portion of the analysis, the gender of the respondent. As hypothesized, men reported having had significantly more input into the marriage decision than did women ($p = .025$ (one-tailed test)).

In the second equation, the variables measuring the age at which the respondent married and the duration of the couple's marriage were added to the estimation, and once again both coefficients are highly significant and in the predicted directions. With the addition of these variables, however, the effects of the respondent's gender, educational attainment, and union order all became non-significant. The disappearance of the effect of gender probably reflects the strong relationship between gender and age at marriage, as roughly 12.7 percent of the women in this sample married when in their early teens, compared with only 1.5 percent of the men.

In the third equation, the dependent variable was regressed on all of the variables measuring the main effects (with the exception of age at marriage), and on interactions between gender and education, and between gender and marital duration. Age at marriage was dropped from this final estimation because of its correlation with gender. Given the revisions to the model, the gender of the respondent reemerged as a strongly significant variable, indicating that women have decision-making scores up to 50 percentage points lower than those of men. In addition, the interaction between gender and educational attainment is significant and positive; improvements in the level of education do appear to have been of greater benefit to women than to men in this sample. This is not surprising. Across cohorts women generally complete fewer years of schooling than do their husbands, so each additional increment is likely to be of disproportionate benefit to them.

TABLE 5.6:   FACTORS AFFECTING PERCEPTIONS OF INPUT INTO
THE MARRIAGE DECISION (MALES AND FEMALES)   (Unstandardized Coefficients)

Independent Variables Equation	1	2	3
Education:			
Respondent's	.043**	.009	-.012
Respondent's father's	.082**	.084**	.162**
Gender of respondent (1=female, 0=male)	-.222*	-.149	-.509**
Interactions:			
Gender with education	n.a.	n.a.	.051**
Gender with marital duration	n.a.	n.a.	.001
Union order	.233*	.132	.263**
Size of community	-.125	.181	.109
Age at marriage	n.a.	.025**	n.a.
Marital duration	n.a.	-.031**	-.039**
Constant	3.557**	4.821**	5.166**
R Square	.07	.15	.14
Number of cases	805	805	805

One-tailed tests of significance: * indicates significance at the .05 level; ** indicates significance at
the .01 level; n.a. indicates variables not entered in
equations.

The variable measuring the level of education achieved by the respondent's father is again significant, and again positive. The more schooling he completed, the more input his daughter or son had into the marriage decision. The direct effect of the length of time spent in the current union remains strong and negative, again indicating that respondents of both genders had more input into marriage decisions made more recently than into those made longer age. At the same time, however, the interaction between gender and marital duration is not significant. The view that change over time has been of greater benefit to women than to men must therefore be largely discounted in the context of the Javanese marriage decision.

SUMMARY

In conclusion, all of the hypotheses investigated in this chapter have gained some support. In general, the variables selected as predictors of decision-making power explain more of the variance in the responses of the wives than they do for the husbands, but even so, some fairly consistent results emerge for both spouses. In each phase of analysis, with the wife alone, husband alone, or the two combined, marital duration and the educational attainment of the appropriate fathers are strong predictors of the respondents' input into the marriage decision. Other findings that are consistent throughout, but that are gender-specific, include the importance of the size of the community in which the respondent lived prior to marriage for women, and age at marriage for men.

Incremental increases in schooling are found to be of greater benefit to the decision making power of women than to that of their husbands, yet there is no significant interaction between gender and marital duration. As a result, any increase in the amount of control Javanese individuals have had over decisions about whom they might marry must be said to have affected men and women about equally to this point.

NOTES

1. Smith's (1982) study of Indonesian marriage patterns suggests that divorce and remarriage are common in Java and Bali. Using data from the national intercensal population survey in 1976, he demonstrates that among ever-married women married fewer than five years prior to the survey, 20 percent were listed as divorced or separated by the time of the survey. Of those women, 35 percent had already married. Among women married 15-19 years prior to the survey, 38 percent were divorced or separated, and 85 percent of that group had remarried.

2. While community of residence prior to marriage and the education of the woman's father remained significant in this equation, the effects of the wife's level of education and of her age at marriage weakened substantially and became non-significant (p in both cases = .06, one-tailed test). As has already been mentioned, it is likely that those who were married at older ages tend to be members of more recent mariage cohorts; (the correlation between age at marriage and marital duration is -.518). Of additional interest is the fact that when marital duration is included in the estimation, the variable measuring union order regains significance (p = .05). While the effect of union order is weakened by the inclusion of the age at marriage variable, the addition of marital duration suggests significant variation on union order within categories of the duration variable that were not evident across categories. Why this is the case is not clear. It may be due, in part, to differences in the timing of first and higher-order marriages between cohorts.

3. Evidence provided by McNicoll and Singarimbun (1983), suggests that that may indeed by the case. Gender differences in age at marriage narrowed considerably between 1961 and 1979, with Java being one of the locations in which the change was most pronounced.

6

Post-Marriage Migration and the Status of Women

In following the previous chapter's assessment of individual inputs into the marriage decision, the central objective of this chapter is to investigate the determinants of women's overall decision-making power within the household once they are married. Some of the factors that affected input into the choice of a marriage partner, such as the educational attainment of the respondent and the amount of time spent in the current union, are expected to continue to influence family decision-making processes throughout the reproductive years.

In addition, factors such as mobility or migration at or soon after marriage, and the amount of contact that is maintained with the parents of either spouse once the marital union is entered, are also predicted to affect levels of intra-household status. As has been noted, frequent contact between the couple and the parents on either side of the family is expected to lower the wife's status within the household, compared to cases in which less regular contact takes place. Not unrelated is the view that the relocation of both spouses within the first four years of marriage should raise the wife's decision-making power within the family. If the couple's mobility at marriage requires an exogamous move for the woman, however, the disruption of her social ties may override the benefits of the move and have a negative effect on her status.

Stated more formally, and given the information presented in Chapters 2 and 3, the following hypotheses are suggested.

6.1) The residential relocation of both spouses after marriage will result in higher intra-household status for the wife compared to cases in which neither spouse moves, or in which only one relocates.

6.2) Women who maintain frequent contact with either or both sets of parents will have lower intra-household status than will women who do not maintain frequent contact with parents on either side of the family.

6.3) If a woman's residential relocation after marriage requires that she move outside of her village, her intra-household status will decrease compared to women who do not change villages.

83

TABLE 6.1: MOBILITY AFTER MARRIAGE BY GENDER

Mobility Measure	Gender of Respondents % of Males	% of Females
Percent of sample:		
who moved	61.9	72.3
who did not move	38.1	27.7
Total percent	100.0	100.0
Of those who moved, timing in relation to marriage:		
Within 4 years	81.1	82.1
After 4 years	18.9	17.9
Total among movers	100.0	100.0
Of those who moved, type of move:		
Endogamous move	58.5	49.6
Exogamous move	41.5	50.4
Total among movers	100.0	100.0
Total number	394	394

POST-MARRIAGE MOBILITY

Data on patterns of post-marriage mobility are presented in Table 6.1. The data indicate that most of the individuals surveyed did, in fact, change their places of residence once they were married. In addition, most conformed to the norm whereby relocation takes place within the first four years of marriage. Roughly 62 percent of the males and 72 percent of the females had experienced a post-wedding move by the time of the survey, and of those, 81.1 percent of the men and 82.1 percent of the women moved within the first four years.

As expected, most respondents lived with their parents prior to marriage. Among the women in this sample 91.9 percent shared a residence with their parents before they married, while 80.7 percent of the men did the same. Although a slight majority of couples surveyed (56.3 percent) established households separate from either set of parents soon after their marriages, post-nuptial co-residence with parents or in-laws was also common; 43.7 percent of female respondents claimed to have lived with one or the other set of parents after they were married. Of those women, more stayed with their own parents than with their in-laws; 30.1 percent reported living with their own family, compared with 13.6 percent who stayed with the husband's family. Data on patterns of co-residence are presented in Table 6.2.

Among the women who moved after marriage, about half moved beyond the borders of their villages, while 41.5 percent of the husbands made an exogamous move. Of the women who changed villages, 25.2 percent moved directly into the home of their in-laws, while only 12.8 percent of women who moved within their own villages, did the same.

PARENTAL CONTACT

Whether or not a move occurred, however, and if so whether or not the move involved inter-village relocation, most respondents (male and female) continued to maintain regular contact with their parents. Roughly one quarter of all couples reported visiting with parents on both sides of the family at least weekly, and over 46 percent saw the parents of either the husband (21.3 percent) or the wife (24.9 percent) at least once a week. The remaining 28.7 percent of the couples reported no weekly visits with the parents of either spouse.

Table 6.3 provides information about the amount of contact that was maintained between individual respondents and each surviving parent at the time of the survey. The data demonstrate that visitation patterns in which parental contact is highly infrequent are rare in rural Java; fewer than 12 percent of the individuals in any given category reported seeing their mothers or fathers less than once a month. Men and women were about equally unlikely to visit their parents only sporadically. Indeed, the highest percentages of respondents in all groups were those who visited

86

TABLE 6.3: FREQUENCY OF CONTACT WITH SURVIVING PARENTS:
PERCENT DISTRIBUTION

Frequency of Visits with Parent	Wife's Parents Mother	Father	Husband's Parents Mother	Father
More than once a week	53.6	45.1	70.0	68.2
About once a week	9.2	10.7	5.5	6.6
2 or 3 times per month	9.1	10.7	5.1	6.0
About once every month	17.5	16.5	3.3	7.9
Less than once a month	10.6	11.0	11.1	11.3
Estimated Average number of visits per month	5.7	5.0	6.8	6.7
Total percent	100	100	100	100
Total number	274	206	217	151

TABLE 6.2: FEMALE RESIDENCE WITH IN-LAWS AND OWN
PARENTS BY MOBILITY BEHAVIOR

Mobility Behavior	After Marriage, the Percentage Living With: In-laws	Own parents	Number in Category
Woman did not move	n.a.	91.9	109
Moved within village	12.8	5.7	141
Total remaining in original village	7.2	43.2	250
Moved to new village	25.2	6.5	139
Total co-residing	13.6	30.1	389

their parents more often than once a week.

Both wives and husbands maintained roughly the same amount of contact with surviving mothers as they did with their surviving fathers. While slight differences appear to exist favoring visits with mothers among the women surveyed, differences between men's visits to their mothers and fathers appear to be negligible.

Some more pronounced gender differences in visitation patterns can also be observed, however; men were much more likely than women to see their parents more than once a week, while women were more apt than men to visit with their parents only about once a month. Despite the greater likelihood that couples would co-reside with the parents of the bride than with those of the groom after marriage, it thus appears as though, overall, more regular contact is maintained with the parents of husbands. That, in combination with observed gender differences in inter-village movement, suggests that couples who do establish independent residences may eventually settle closer to the home of the husband's family than to that of the wife.

As a rule, the patterns of mobility and family visitation reported in this sample thus conform to the patterns described in earlier studies of Java (Jay, 1969; Nag, 1980). Many couples establish households separate from extended family members upon or soon after marriage, but then continue to maintain close contact with their parents. Among women who relocate after marriage, roughly half move within the village, while the other half move elsewhere. Those who do establish a residence with the parents of either spouse are more likely to live with the parents of the wife than with those of the husband.

THE INTRA-HOUSEHOLD STATUS OF WOMEN

The distributions of the dependent variables measuring the respondents' perceptions of their decision-making power within the family, together with information about the means and variances of the variables, are presented in Table 6.4. The means for men and women are generally consistent across different types of decisions; although female averages are slightly higher in all cases than are those of the husbands as a group, the differences are slight.

The data demonstrate that most men and women in rural Java feel they have at least an equal say about how major household decisions are resolved. Mean scores range from 3.3 for men and 3.4 among women in the decision about adopting contraception, to 3.7 for men and 4.0 for women in the decision about control over personal income. In fact, fewer than four percent of all respondents claimed to have had less than a 50-50 share in deciding how their incomes would be spent, and fewer than six percent felt they had less than an equal share in making the decision to discontinue childbearing. A slightly higher proportion (12.2 percent of women and 9.2 percent of men) felt they had little or no control over the decision to use contraception.

Men are more likely than women to feel that they had total control over the contraceptive decision, while women are more likely than men to fall slightly lower on the continuum, in the group who believe that they had a majority, but not complete control over the contraception decision. The highest percentages of both males and females are found in the third group, those who claimed to have shared about equally in the decision-making process.

TABLE 6.4: PERCENT DISTRIBUTIONS OF VARIABLES MEASURING DECISION-MAKING POWER

	Type of Decision					
Amount of Power	Stop Childbearing		Use Contraception		Control Resources	
	Women	Men	Women	Men	Women	Men
Total Control	12.9	12.7	8.2	10.6	37.6	24.7
Most Control	38.1	32.0	37.2	24.0	31.9	28.4
Equal Control	43.9	49.8	42.4	56.2	29.2	43.2
Less Control	2.6	1.9	6.6	4.1	0.3	1.6
No Control	2.5	3.6	5.6	5.1	1.0	2.1
Total Percent	100	100	100	100	100	100
Number of Cases	278	275	231	217	295	384
Mean	3.6	3.5	3.4	3.3	4.0	3.7
Variance	.71	.76	.87	.82	.77	.85

Similarly, roughly equal proportions of husbands and wives reported that they alone controlled the decision to stop having children, but more men than women believe they shared equally in the decision, while more wives than husbands claimed that they played the dominant role (i.e., had more input into the decision than did the other(s) involved). The fact that this pattern parallels the one observed for the contraception decision is not surprising, especially where contraception is used more for stopping than for spacing pregnancies.

The pattern of control over income expenditures is more striking, however. Among women, 37.6 percent reported having had complete control over decisions about how their incomes would be spent, while only 24.7 percent of the males believed they had complete control over the allocation of their own earnings. Further, although a full 43.2 percent of the men said they shared about equally with others in making decisions about income expenditures, only 29.2 percent of the women believed they belonged in that category.

As a rule, these data indicate that decisions are made among the couples in this sample much as earlier writers have suggested they are made among the Javanese in general. Women have a good deal to say about how important household decisions are made, especially those involving financial matters, and the decision-making process appears to be largely cooperative in nature.

MULTIVARIATE ANALYSIS

To examine the relationships between the dependent variables and the predictors of interest, a number of regression equations have been estimated. Included among them are estimations in which constructed measures of overall decision-making power among women and men are utilized.

In the first set of equations, the indicators of the woman's decision-making power are regressed on the mobility and contact variables, the measures of education and income, the wife's input into the marriage decision, and the controls for age at marriage and marital duration. The dependent variable in the first equation is the composite measure of the woman's status. In the second equation, it is her level of input into decisions about the ever-use of contraception. In the third, the dependent variable measures the woman's input into the decision to discontinue childbearing, and in the fourth, the focus is on the decisions surrounding income expenditures. The results are presented in Table 6.5.

In all four equations, the reference category for the first set of mobility variables contains the group believed to be normative in rural Java as a whole, the one in which both spouses move within the first four years of marriage. That set of variables was expected to demonstrate that women in the reference category fare better in terms of their decision-making power than do women in any other group. While almost all of the

TABLE 6.5: DETERMINANTS OF THE WIFE'S DECISION-MAKING POWER WITHIN THE FAMILY

Independent Variables	Unstandardized Coefficients			
	Total (Standardized)	Use B.C.	Stop Fertility	Control Resources
Mobility After Marriage:				
Both move after				
4 yrs. (a)	-.144	-.096	-.062	-.048
Husband only (a)	-.127	-.364**	-.108	.024
Wife only (a)	-.089	-.148	-.016	.117
Neither moves (a)	-.398**	-.558***	-.245	-.087
Wife changes vill. (1st 4 yrs) (b)	-.083	-.374***	-.234**	-.082
Wife changes vill. later (b)	.288	.040	.600***	-.198
Parental Contact (c):				
Both sides - 1+/week	-.223*	-.191	-.265**	-.426***
Wife's side seen 1+/week	.133	-.109	-.021	-.234
Husband's side seen 1+/wk.	.041	.025	.121	-.159
Wife's input into marriage decision	.067**	.108***	.108***	.001
Wife's education	-.011	.033	-.004	.013
Husband's education	.027**	-.010	n.a.	n.a.
Wife's income (ln)	.103 **	.014	.032***	-.043
Husband's (ln)	.030	n.a.	.009	.021***
Age at marriage	-.008	n.a.	n.a.	n.a.
Marital duration	.022	.002	-.002	.001
Constant	-1.489**	3.113***	3.083***	4.361***
R Square	.28	.10	.10	.06
Number of Cases	383	229	274	292

(a) Reference category contains couples in which both spouses moved within first four years of marriage. (b) Reference category refers to women who have not moved since marriage. (c) Reference category contains couples who do not have frequent contact with either set of parents.

* Significant at the .10 level; ** Significant at the .05 level; *** Significant at the .01 level. (1-tailed test of significance).

coefficients in the four equations prove to be negative, only the variable comparing couples in which neither spouse moved with those in the reference category is found to be a significant determinant of the woman's overall decision-making power.

This most likely reflects the relative inability of young women, who along with their husbands remained in one place before and after marriage, to control central aspects of their lives. In the majority of these cases one spouse is apt to have moved in with the other spouse's family before their marriage took place. Intergenerational decision-making dynamics, and not inter-spousal ones, therefore appear to be most important when considering the relationship between this measure of residential mobility and the overall status of women within the household in rural Java.

Similarly, only the variable comparing couples in which neither spouse moved and couples among whom only the husband moved with those in the reference category, significantly predict the woman's ability to control the contraception decision. When only the husband moved after the wedding, again commonly into the wife's parents' home, the woman's ability to control decisions about the use of birth control suffered considerably compared to cases in which both spouses moved. Some support is thus attained for Hypothesis 6.1.

Whether or not a woman's post-marriage relocation involved migration to another village is also of importance in predicting her power within the household. If she moved to a new village within the first four years of marriage, her ability to control decisions about the adoption of contraception and the discontinuation of childbearing diminished substantially (by 23 percentage points and 37 percentage points respectively). Conversely, women who did not make an exogamous move played more dominant roles in making contraceptive and childbearing decisions. As has been argued, the negative impact of the longer distance move was probably the result of the removal of the migrants from important social networks. Support is therefore also attained for Hypothesis 6.3.

In the case of the childbearing decision, however, it is found that if the inter-village relocation occurred after the couple had been married for more than four years, the move then significantly enhanced the women's decision-making power (by 60 percentage points). This suggests that while new brides may benefit from an adjustment period during which they remain in proximity to close social contacts, once they become accustomed to married life those contacts diminish in importance. Further, since exogamous moves that take place after four years are less apt to be directed toward the home of in-laws and more toward independent residences, later inter-village mobility can be of particular benefit to women as it improves their control over childbearing decisions.

Whether or not a move occurs at all, however, and regardless of the timing and direction of the move, the actual amount of contact the couple maintains with both spouses' parents also proves to be central to the decision-making process. In this sample, wives who, along with their husbands, saw parents on both sides of the family at least once a week had much lower overall decision-making power (by 22 percentage points) than did those with no regular contact with either set of parents. This effect is significant in the equations estimating women's input into the decisions about childbearing and resource control as well, and it is particularly strong in the latter. Maintaining less frequent contact with both spouse's parents improves a woman's ability to influence decisions about the allocation of her own income by almost 43 percentage points. Support is therefore also found for Hypothesis 6.2.

It has been noted that in regions such as Central Java, where marriages are frequently arranged, the ability of women to influence decisions about their marriages is likely to be associated with their power to control later household decisions as well. That is found to be the case here. The coefficient for the variable measuring the amount of input the women in this sample perceived themselves to have had into the marriage decision is positive and highly significant in all but the resource control equation. This is as expected and may reflect variations in levels of tradition versus modernity in the backgrounds of the women surveyed. Those who have come from more traditional backgrounds may be more likely to allow others to guide household decisions over the life course, while those who have been exposed to more modern influences may be less willing to relinquish control.

If so, the level of education attained by the woman would be expected to be closely associated with the variable measuring her input into the marriage decision. That appears to be the case only in the contraception equation, however. When the variable measuring input into the marriage decision is excluded from that estimation, the coefficient for the woman's level of schooling is found to be significant and positive (data not presented). In all other estimations her educational attainment proves to be unrelated to her decision-making power.

The income variables, on the other hand, are better predictors of the woman's autonomy. Female earnings coefficients are positive and significant in measuring both the woman's overall decision-making power and her input into the childbearing decision. The more income the wife makes, the more she has to say about important household matters. Some support is thus provided for the argument that increased access to resources enhances women's control over central elements in their lives, as well as for the view that transfers of western or "modern" ideas, such as those espousing increased status for women, are apt to accrue first to higher socioeconomic status groups.

If that is true, however, it is somewhat surprising that this variable fails to predict the woman's input into the contraception decision. Higher earnings were expected to play a central role in allowing women greater access to information and services, and therefore in allowing them greater input into contraceptive decisions. That is not the case when the other variables are controlled, possibly because the earnings effects are offset by the intervention of government family planning advisors interested in increasing contraceptive prevalence. Low income women may be among those least able to resist official pressure to adopt a method of family planning.

Also not anticipated was the finding that the actual amount of income the wife earns is of no statistical importance in enhancing her control over decisions governing its use. Instead, what is significant is the amount of money her husband brings home; the higher his income, the more she has to say about how the money she earns will be spent. While at very low levels of household income every increment must be allocated to meet basic needs, higher levels allow for more discretion in targeting consumption and investments. That the wife's earnings are less important than her husband's in this process is probably at least partly because many women seek employment in the cash economy only when it becomes necessary to supplement the low earnings of their husbands (Mangkuprawira, 1981).

Finally, if female status has been improving over time in Indonesia, it should follow that the women who had been married the longest should be those with the least in-house decision-making power. In our sample, however, that is not found to be the case. Any effect of change over time as measured through marital duration is therefore probably offset by the fact that older women tend to have higher status within the family than do younger brides. Older women have had more time to accrue some power, and they have had more time to establish independent households as well.

Since the two spouses are not the only ones involved in making many of these household decisions, as parents often continue to influence the decision-making process long after the couple is married, the variables that most influence the husband's perceptions of his decision-making power must also be examined.

It might be predicted that the variables that are most relevant to an inter-spousal dynamic, and that have a significant effect on the power of the wives, should have the opposite effect on the decision-making power of the husbands, while the variables that pertain more to the inter-generational dynamic should affect the two spouses similarly. The results presented in Table 6.6 provide only very limited support for this argument. For example, all of the mobility variables and all of the parental contact variables are statistically unimportant in predicting the overall decision-making power of the men in this sample. The amount of input males perceive themselves to have in making major household decisions is thus unaffected by the timing or distance of post-marriage migration, or by the amount of contact that is maintained with the parents on either or both sides of the family.

A certain element of the intergenerational dynamic does appear to play a role in the decision-making process, however. As was the case among women, husbands who feel they had a considerable amount of input into the marriage decision also tend to be those who feel they have had substantial control over subsequent decisions.

In the inter-spousal dynamic, it is found that while the education variables fail to predict the husband's relative status within the household, the income variables do significantly affect his decision-making power. The higher his earnings, the greater his control over household decisions.

TABLE 6.6: DETERMINANTS OF THE HUSBAND'S DECISION-MAKING POWER WITHIN THE FAMILY

Independent Variable	Unstandardized Coefficients
Mobility After Marriage:	
Both move after 4 yrs. (a)	.365
Husband only moves (a)	.214
Wife only moves (a)	.191
Neither one moves (a)	-.008
Wife changes village-1st 4 yrs. (b)	.020
Wife changes village later (b)	.064
Parental Contact:	
Freq. of contact w/ wife's mother	n.a.
Freq. of contact w/ husb.'s mother	n.a.
Both sides seen 1+/week (c)	.080
Wife's side seen 1+/week (c)	-.058
Husband's side seen 1+/wk. (c)	.137
Husband's input into marriage decision	.171***
Wife's decision-making power	.775***
Wife's education	.013
Husband's education	-.004
Wife's income (logged)	-.101***
Husband's income	.089*
Marital duration	.030***
Constant	-1.572***

R Square	.41
Number of Cases	380

(a) Reference category contains couples in which both spouses moved within first four years of marriage. (b) Reference category refers to women who have not moved since marriage. (c) Reference category contains couples who do not have frequent contact with either set of parents. *Significant at the .05 level; ** Significant at the .01 level; *** Significant at the .001 level. (2-tailed test of significance).

Higher earnings on the part of their wives, however, yield lower levels of decision-making power for male respondents; the less their wives earn, the more power the men feel they can exert in major household decisions. This supports the view that access to resources is important in order for women to be able to exercise some control in inter-personal relationships.

The coefficient for the variable measuring marital duration is also highly significant and positive. The longer a couple has been married, the more control the husband feels he has over major household decisions. It has been argued that couples married longer ago are apt to be those characterized by more traditional patterns of male dominance, and that those married more recently should be those among whom more egalitarian relationships should prevail. While that explanation may be plausible, caution must be exercised before relying to heavily on the conclusion above. It could also be, for example, that males at higher marital durations have gained power vis-a-vis their parents. While the positive effect of marital duration is not the result of the fact that older parents are no longer living (since that information would have been picked up in the controls for parental contact), it could reflect the fact that once parents become increasingly aged their input into major decisions begins to decline. The positive impact of marital duration upon a husband's ability to control household matters therefore probably arises out of a combination of inter-generational and inter-spousal dynamics.

Finally, it was thought that a control for the composite measure for the wife's perceptions of her decision-making power would provide additional information about how males view their own power. Given the framework within which the husband's responses are analyzed, it would be expected that the more power one spouse believes herself/himself to be able to exercise, the less power the other spouse would probably perceive herself/himself to have. This is not found to be the case, however. Instead, the greater the wife's perceived autonomy within the household, the more power the husband believes himself to have as well.

This may reflect variations in the amount of discussion that takes place on particular topics. If, for example, a given subject is discussed a great deal, any outcome resulting from the conversation may be viewed as a definite decision, rather than as an event that takes place simply by default; if a great deal of conversation is needed to determine a course of action, both spouses may believe that they had a substantial amount of input into the decision in question.

SUMMARY

In summary, some support is found for all three of the hypotheses tested in this chapter. Hypothesis 6.1 predicted that the residential relocation of both spouses within four years of marriage would result in increases in the intra-household status of the wife, compared to cases in which neither spouse moved, only one relocated, or they both moved after more than four years of marriage. The results demonstrate that when neither spouse moves within the first four years, or when only the husband moves, the wife has considerably less input into decisions about initiating contraceptive use than is true when both husband and wife relocate. In addition, when the overall decision-making power of the woman is estimated, her intra-household status is lower in cases in which neither spouse moves than in those in which both relocate within the first four years of their union.

These findings demonstrate that women can gain influence within the household through residential mobility. Because the coefficients remain significant even when the amount of contact that is maintained with parents on both sides of the family is controlled, it is clear that the actual physical relocation of the couple has an independent effect upon the wife's overall decision-making power, as well as on her ability to control the outcome of contraception decisions.

It is also found that if a woman's post-nuptial relocation takes her beyond the borders of her village, her decision-making power suffers compared to women who do not make an exogamous move. This has been argued to be the result of loosening ties with important social networks. The effect is significant for the contraception decision, as well as for the decision about curtailing childbearing. Support is therefore also lent to Hypothesis 6.3. If, on the other hand, the inter-village relocation takes place after the couple has been married for at least four years, the wife's decision-making power is found improve. At that point the importance of initial support systems seems to diminish, while the establishment of an independent residence becomes especially salient in the decision-making process.

In addition to post-marriage mobility, parental contact is a strong predictor of a woman's power to influence decision outcomes. This supports Hypothesis 6.2. When parents on both sides of the family are seen regularly, the wife's intra-familial status suffers compared to cases in which no regular contact is maintained with parents on either side. This is the case in the estimation of the woman's overall decision-making power, as well as in decisions regarding the discontinuation of childbearing and the allocation of the wife's earnings.

Admittedly, several levels of participation are likely to be involved in these decisions. That is, in fact, assumed to be the case. Although parents may not directly control the final decisions of their children, they are often able to exert a great deal of influence over the thought processes that lead up to them, as well as over the contexts in which the decisions are made and outcomes implemented. This is particularly true as long as sons and daughters continue to co-reside with their parents, or to see them several times a week. Indeed, the importance of the intergenerational dynamic in the process is confirmed in this analysis, as previous input into the decision to marry is found to be significant and positive in four of the five equations estimated; the more input either respondent had into the decision to marry, the more control she or he is then able to exert in later household decisions as well.

To conclude, migration at or after marriage, the amount of contact that is maintained with parents on both sides of the family, prior decision-making power, and to a certain extent levels of socioeconomic status, all operate across cohorts to influence the amount of control women in Central Java are able to exert over important family decisions. Among men in this sample, perceptions of their own decision-making power are best predicted by the length of time spent in the current marital union, the cash earnings of both spouses, and the amount of input their wives have into household decisions.

7

Contraception and Fertility

In this portion of the analysis, the relationships between the status of women within the Javanese family and their contraceptive use and fertility behavior are assessed. The information presented in Chapter 2 suggested that women with higher status within the family should be more likely to use contraception and to exhibit low levels of fertility than should women with less autonomy. In addition, women with high status on a second dimension, that which compares individuals across households on indicators such as education and income, should be more likely to be ever-users of birth control and to have smaller families than should women with lower status on that dimension. Specifically, the following hypotheses are suggested:

(7.1) Women who have high intra-household status will be more likely to be ever-users of contraception than will women with low status within the household.

(7.2) Women who have high intra-household status will have lower fertility than will women with low status within the household.

(7.3) Women who have high extra-household status will be more likely to be ever-users of contraception than will women with low status on that dimension.

(7.4) Women who have high extra-household status will have lower fertility than will women with low status on that dimension.

As was discussed in Chapter 3, over the past twenty years the government of Indonesia has been firmly committed to bringing about reductions in overall fertility rates by increasing contraceptive use and efficacy throughout the country. Of the major islands, Java now has the lowest total fertility rate (the 1980 TFR = 3.89), and of the provinces on that island, Central Java has been moderately successful compared to the other provinces; (the 1980 TFR = 4.08).

The percent distribution of children ever born (CEB) to the women in this sample is displayed in Table 7.1.

TABLE 7.1:   PERCENT DISTRIBUTION OF CHILDREN EVER BORN

Number of Childen Ever Born	Percent
0	4.1
1-2	25.9
3-4	30.9
5-6	18.5
7 or more	20.6
Total	100.0
Mean	4.13

As is true throughout Central Java, fertility among the women surveyed remains quite high. The mean number of children born to them thus far is 4.13. On the other hand, contraception has also been widely used among the sampled women; 58.9 percent claim to be ever-users of birth control. It is therefore not unreasonable to expect that when more recent cohorts have completed their childbearing they will have smaller families, on average, than will the women from older cohorts.

Another reason why this may come to pass is that roughly two thirds of the women surveyed believe that the ideal number of children they could have is three or fewer. Data on ideal family size are presented in Table 7.2. The mean number of children women consider to be ideal is 3.4, the median is 3.0, and most women (86.7 percent) believe that having between two and four is optimal.[1]

As has been noted, in order for couples to plan smaller families, the use of contraception has been strongly encouraged throughout Central Java and the nation as a whole. Data on relative preferences for particular contraceptive methods in the province of Central Java, as well as in Kabupaten Sukoharjo, are presented in Table 7.3.

The pill is clearly the most popular program method utilized at either the *kabupaten* or province level, although IUDs are also widely used. Together, the two methods account for over 80 percent of the non-traditional contraceptive use within both the lower administrative district and the province. Injections and condoms are slightly less prevalent in Sukoharjo than in the rest of Central Java, while sterilization is relatively more common in the *kabupaten* than in the province as a whole.

TABLE 7.2:   DISTRIBUTION OF IDEAL NUMBER OF CHILDREN

Ideal Number of Children	Percent
1-2	17.9
3	48.2
4-5	29.1
6 or more	4.8
Total	100.0
Mean	3.4

TABLE 7.3:   CONTRACEPTIVE METHODS CHOSEN IN SUKOHARJO
AND CENTRAL JAVA AS A WHOLE (1984)

Method Used	Sukoharjo		Central Java	
	Number	Percent	Number	Percent
IUD	27,971	35.76	879,262	30.45
Pill	43,251	55.29	475,516	51.09
Condom	2,604	3.33	207,435	7.18
Sterilization	3,424	4.38	88,272	3.06
Injection	978	1.25	237,382	8.22
Total	78,228	100%	2,887,867	100%

Data are from Pusat Jaringan Informasi & Dokumentasi
Program, KB Nasional (1985), pp.129-130.

TABLE 7.4:   CONTRACEPTIVE METHODS CHOSEN FOR FIRST USE
BY VILLAGE

Method	Jombor	Kenep	Manden	Wonorjo	Total
Pill	·13.2	32.0	26.3	39.7	28.1
IUD	38.2	44.0	55.3	23.5	38.0
Condom	3.9	2.0	0.0	2.9	2.6
Injection	9.2	6.0	13.2	11.8	10.0
Male Ster.	0.0	4.0	0.0	1.5	1.3
Fem. Ster.	13.2	6.0	2.6	0.0	6.0
Implant	1.3	0.0	0.0	1.5	0.1
Foam/Jelly	0.0	0.0	0.0	1.5	0.1
Abstinence	9.2	4.0	0.0	1.5	4.3
Traditional	11.8	0.0	0.0	7.3	6.0
Combination (non-trad)	0.0	0.0	2.6	5.9	2.2
Combination (trad. & non-trad).	0.0	2.0	0.0	2.9	1.3
Total	100.0	100.0	100.0	100.0	100.0

Information about the contraceptive choices made by the couples in this sample are presented in Table 7.4. The data indicate that the IUD is the most popular first-use method, followed closely by the pill. Use of injections, female sterilization, traditional methods, and abstinence is somewhat less common, and methods oriented specifically toward males do not tend to be widely accepted as first-use methods.

The relative popularity of many of the different family planning services is fairly consistent across villages. Only in Wonorjo are there more pill acceptors than IUD users, and IUD use is common there nonetheless. The only method that is used fairly frequently in one village and hardly at all elsewhere, is female sterilization. Sterilizations among women accounted for 13.2 percent of all method utilization in Jombor, compared with only six percent in Kenep, 2.6 percent in Manden, and none at all in Wonorjo.

The evidence thus suggests that the government's programs have met with some success in all four villages. Of the 58.9 percent of the women who claimed to be ever-users of birth control, only 8.2 percent used traditional methods (including abstinence) when they first used contraception.

TABLE 7.5:   PERCENT DISTRIBUTION OF CONTRACEPTIVE USE
BY EDUCATION OF EACH SPOUSE

Male Educatiom (years)	Contraceptive Users	Non-Users	Female Education (years)	Contraceptive Users	Non-Users
0	45.1	54.9	0	45.3	54.7
1-3	45.1	54.9	1-3	56.9	43.1
4-6	56.8	43.2	4-6	64.2	35.8
7+	79.5	20.5	7+	80.3	19.7

Chi-square=31.06; d.f.=3; significance = .000.   Chi-square=23.83; d.f.=3; significance = .000.

VARIABLES ASSOCIATED WITH CONTRACEPTIVE USE

Not surprisingly, many of the variables commonly cited as predictors of contraception are also related to the ever-use of birth control among the women in this sample. For example, there is a significant bivariate association between the educational attainment levels of both spouses and whether or not they have ever used a method of contraception. (See Table 7.5). As the number of years of schooling completed by husbands and wives increases, so does the likelihood that they will have used some form of family planning at some point during their marriage.

Similarly, the size of the community in which the wife lived prior to marriage is also associated with contraceptive behavior; as the size of that community increases, so does the likelihood that she and her husband will have ever adopted some form of birth control. A full 92.9 percent of the women who lived in cities of 250,000 or more prior to their marriages were found to be ever-users of contraception, compared to only 57.8 percent of those who lived in smaller urban or rural places.[2]

TABLE 7.6: PERCENT DISTRIBUTIONS OF CONTRACEPTIVE
USE BY FREQUENCY OF DISCUSSION BETWEEN SPOUSES

Discussion Frequency	Contraceptive Users	Row %	Contraceptive Non-Users	Row %
Never	16.5	27.1	63.4	72.9
Not often	18.2	72.4	9.9	27.6
Somewhat often	38.5	75.4	18.0	24.6
Often	21.2	84.5	5.6	15.5
Very often	5.6	72.2	3.1	27.8
Totals	100.0		100.0	

Chi-square = 93.03; d.f.=4; significance = .000

Also correlated with contraceptive use is the desire for additional children. Among women in this sample, contraceptive use was much more common among couples who wished to have no more children than it was among those who were still hoping to continue their childbearing. Although 49 couples wanting additional children reported having used a method of family planning at some point, most contraceptors were those who wished to prevent rather than space further births. Among ever-users of birth control, 78.9 percent claimed to want no more children, compared to 21.1 percent who hoped to continue childbearing.

Equally important is whether or not spouses are able to communicate about family planning options. In this survey, information was gathered about whether or not, and if so to what extent such conversations took place. As expected, bivariate tests demonstrate that more frequent discussions about family planning and birth control are positively associated with the use of contraception. Results are presented in Table 7.6.

While the amount of discussion that takes place between spouses may be one indicator of inter-spousal dynamics, the variable of primary interest here remains the decision-making power of the woman. Given the information presented in Chapters 2 and 3, it was predicted that women with higher intra-household status would be more likely to use contraception than would women with little control over household decisions. Contrary to expectations, however, the relationship between ever-use of contraception and the woman's status within the family, as measured by her input into decisions about how her income is spent, is not significant. Data are presented in Table 7.7.

TABLE 7.7: CONTRACEPTIVE USE BY THE WIFE'S DECISION-MAKING POWER WITHIN THE HOUSEHOLD (Measured by Resource Control Variable)

Decision-Making Power (5=high, 1=low)	Percent Using Contraception
1.0	100.0
2.0	100.0
3.0	61.6
4.0	63.4
5.0	51.4

Chi-square=6.46; d.f.=4; significance level=.168

TABLE 7.8: CONTRACEPTIVE USE BY MOBILITY AFTER MARRIAGE

Who Moves	Percent Ever-Using Contraception
Neither spouse	28.1
Husband only	59.0
Wife only	60.7
Both spouses	63.9

Chi-square = 14.54; d.f.= 3; significance level=.002.

Why this is the case is not certain. It does not, for example, reflect variation in the use of modern versus traditional methods of contraception at different levels of decision-making power. That possibility was explored but rejected. What is more likely is that women who have very little power within the household are also those most easily pressured by local leaders or other family members to use contraception. That possibility was briefly discussed in Chapter 6.

It is also conceivable that the women with the highest intra-household autonomy tend to be those with the most education and thus those most recently out of school. As such, they would almost by definition be members of the youngest cohorts and presumably those who have not yet reached their fertility targets. Where contraception is used primarily to prevent rather than space further births that explanation could have some merit.

Finally, although it was expected that the mobility variables would operate primarily through the decision-making variable to influence contraceptive use, the bivariate association presented in Table 7.8 suggests that there is also a direct relationship between post-marriage mobility and contraception.[3] Only 28.1 percent of the couples among whom neither spouse moved after marriage were ever-users of contraception, compared to 59 percent of those in which only the husband moved and 60.7 percent of those among whom only the wife moved. When both spouses relocated after their marriage, 63.9 percent of the couples reported having ever adopted some form of birth control. This is not surprising; in some of the cases in which neither spouse moved they were probably not yet co-residing, while in other instances, one spouse was likely to have joined the other by moving in with in-laws prior to marriage. In cases in which the wife was the only mover, contraceptive usage was just slightly higher than was true if the husband was the only mover. This is probably because in a few of the cases in which only the wife moved, she moved into an independent household established by her husband prior to their marriage.[4]

MULTIVARIATE DETERMINANTS OF CONTRACEPTIVE USE

Given the complexity of the relationships between these variables, multivariate analyses were also undertaken to examine the determinants of contraceptive use among the women of this sample. Results are presented in Table 7.9. Since the dependent variable (contraceptive use or non-use) is dichotomous, a logistic regression was estimated.[5]

The data demonstrate that many of the associations described thus far are sustained even when all of the other variables are controlled. For example, compared to cases in which neither spouse had moved, those in which only the husband or the wife had moved, as well as those in which both partners had moved, were all more likely to have ever used contraception. Again, couples in the reference category are probably those who were not yet sharing a residence at the time of the survey, or those

TABLE 7.9: MULTIVARIATE DETERMINANTS OF EVER-USE OF
CONTRACEPTIVES

Independent Variable	Logistic Regression Coefficients
Mobility Variables:	
Both spouses move	1.59**
Wife only moves	1.78***
Husband only moves	1.96***
Desire additional children (1—yes, 0—no)	-1.73***
Frequency of contraception discussion	0.65***
Wife's decision-making power (Resource control)	-0.44***
Size of wife's community before marriage (higher score—more urban)	1.15
Wife's education	0.73
Husband's education	0.55
Wife's income (logged) -	0.52*
Married 26 or more years	-0.67*
Married 15 or fewer years	0.76*
Constant	4.11
Number of cases	293

*Significant at the .10 level; ** Significant at the .05
level; ***Significant at the .01 level : Two-tailed test
of significance. (a) Reference group—those married
16-25 years.

who had begun co-residing with one or the other set of in-laws prior to their marriage.

It was thought that they might also be the couples who married the earliest, and therefore probably those from the oldest cohorts. That was found not to be the case through a test of means, however. The ages at marriage of spouses who had not moved were not significantly different from those in the other mobility categories.

The couples who comprise the various mobility categories do vary significantly across groups as to the amount of schooling the wife had attained and the size of her place of residence prior to marriage, however. In cases in which neither spouse moved following marriage, wives were found to have completed an average of 3.2 years of schooling. When only the husband or the wife moved, the wives averaged 3.5 years of education, and in cases in which both spouses moved, women generally attained an average of 4.5 years. This may be one reason why the education variables weakened and became non-significant in the multivariate analysis. Neither the husband's nor the wife's level of schooling successfully predicts contraceptive use or non-use when the other variables are controlled.

TABLE 7.10:   CHILDREN EVER BORN BY LEVEL OF DECISION-MAKING POWER [RESOURCE CONTROL, RESTRICTED SAMPLE]

Level of Decision -making Power	Number of CEB				
	0	1-2	3-4	5-6	7+
Lowest	0.0	33.3	66.7	0.0	0.0
Moderately low	0.0	0.0	0.0	100.0	0.0
Moderate	4.7	26.7	30.2	16.3	22.1
Moderately high	3.2	27.3	33.3	18.1	18.1
Highest	5.4	23.4	32.5	21.6	17.1
Number in column	13	76	95	56	55

A similar pattern is observed for the variable measuring the size of the wife's community prior to marriage. Given our sample, every woman in a union in which neither spouse had moved following their marriage must, by definition, have lived in a rural area before the wedding. Women in unions in which both spouses had moved, were obviously much more likely to have lived in a large urban center. As is true of the education variables, the size of residence variable fails to predict contraceptive use or non-use when the other variables are controlled.

Still very important in predicting contraceptive use is the frequency with which conversations about family planning had taken place between husbands and wives. The more often family planning issues had been discussed, the greater the likelihood that the couple had used some form of birth control during their marriage.

Not surprisingly, the desire for additional children is also a significant predictor of contraceptive use. Women who wanted to continue childbearing were less likely to have used contraception than were those who wanted no more children. Again, this suggests that family planning services are particularly popular among women who wish to curtail further childbearing entirely.

Given past research, it is somewhat more surprising that higher incomes among the sampled women are associated with lower levels of contraceptive use. Additional resources have often been argued to give women more control over household decisions, including those pertaining to reproduction, and to provide them with the means to obtain birth control when it is they who must do the purchasing. In Indonesia, however, aside "from a registration fee charged to most clinic users" contraceptive acceptors have long received services free of charge through the government's family planning program (McNicoll and Singarimbun, 1983:84).

It is also clear that income and actual fertility are positively correlated in many parts of the world (Mueller and Short, 1983). The more income a family earns, the more children they can afford to have, and vice versa. If, as has already been observed, children in Central Java are seen as producing increases in wealth for the family, and if the couple is able to afford the initial investment of an additional child, they will be relatively unlikely to use contraception.[6]

Probably the most plausible explanation for the negative relationship between income and ever-use of contraception in this context is the one offered by McNicoll and Singarimbun (1983). They argue that people at the lowest income levels in Java are most likely to use contraception because 1) they are particularly susceptible to a combination of Malthusian pressures, and 2) because their ability to resist government campaigns to reduce fertility is limited. Freedman et al. (1981) have found a curvilinear effect of income upon contraception in Indonesia, and have posited similar explanations for the behavior of the lower income groups.

The impact of marital duration upon contraceptive use is more straightforward. Everything else being equal, the longer the couple has been married, the less likely they are ever to have utilized a method of birth control. Women who had been married 15 or fewer years at the time of the survey were significantly more likely to have ever used a family planning method than were those married 16-25 years, while women married longer than 25 years were, in turn, significantly less likely to have been ever-users. That is not surprising. Most of the women who were married longest are from earlier birth cohorts, are more traditional in general, and are less apt to have been targeted for family planning programs than are those who were married more recently.

Finally, the variable measuring the woman's power to control decisions about income expenditures has a negative impact on contraceptive use. The effect is independent of the woman's marital duration and her desire for additional children, variables mentioned earlier as possible mediating factors in the relationship between intra-household status and contraception. In addition, if the sample is split by levels of marital duration or by parity to see whether or not the association varies within categories of either of those variables, the relationship remains.[7] As was the case for the variable measuring the woman's income, it is therefore likely that the negative effect of women's decision-making power reflects the fact that those with the least power within the family are also those most easily influenced by government officials hoping to increase contraceptive use.

FACTORS AFFECTING FERTILITY

When the determinants of children ever born are examined, the effect of the intra-household status of the woman is found to disappear entirely. Data measuring the bivariate relationship between women's decision-making power and their fertility are presented in Table 7.10. Chi-square tests indicate that the association between the two variables is not significant (p=.90). Again, this runs counter to expectations and suggests that either the indicator of women's status is not adequate, or that women's decision-making power is simply not relevant to fertility behavior in the Indonesian context. Both may be true to varying degrees.[8]

It is also possible that the effect of women's status on fertility in Indonesia is an indirect one, operating primarily through contraceptive use or non-use, or through a number of other variables to influence reproductive behavior. If so, however, the path through which it operates remains ambiguous. For example, women with higher levels of decision-making power are less likely to be ever-users of contraception, but more apt to state a preference for smaller families than are women with lower status. The indirect effects of status may therefore cancel one another out.

Perhaps most salient is an issue that was raised in Chapter 2. It has been argued that one problem with many analyses that focus on women's status and fertility is that it is almost invariably assumed that women want to limit their childbearing, but that their husbands do not. While that is not assumed to be the case in this analysis, it is useful to examine the extent to which the reproductive goals of the spouses in this sample actually coincide. Results are presented in Table 7.11. The data indicate that there is, in fact, very little disagreement between husbands and wives in Java as to their family size ideals. The majority of cases (261 couples, or 66.2 percent) fall somewhere on the diagonal, indicating that among almost two thirds of the respondents, there is exact agreement between the woman and her husband as to their reproductive preferences.

Where disagreement does exist it tends not to be extreme, and the split is fairly even between cases in which men desire larger families than do their wives, and those in which women desire larger families than do their husbands. In 16.5 percent of the cases, men favor having more children than do women, while in 17.3 percent of the cases, the reverse is true. This suggests that the topic may be one that is often discussed, and that as a result, men and women often come to a shared understanding of what their reproductive targets will be.

TABLE 7.11: HUSBANDS' AND WIFES' FAMILY SIZE IDEALS

| Wife's Ideal | 0 | Husband's Ideal Family Size | | | |
		1-2	3-4	5-6	7 or More
1-2	0.0	7.3	8.6	1.0	1.0
3-4	1.0	10.4	52.3	3.3	2.0
5-6	0.3	1.0	2.8	4.8	1.0
7+	0.0	1.0	1.0	0.3	1.8

Total Percentage - 100.

Chi-square - 406.98; d.f.-80; significance-.000.

Aside from the lack of association between the woman's decision-making power and her fertility, most of the results of the other bivariate tests are as expected. There are, for example, significant inverse linear relationships between children ever born and the educational attainment levels of both women and men. Results are displayed in Table 7.12.

Similarly, marital duration is strongly associated with fertility (p=.000; r=.678). As the number of years a couple has been married increases, so does the number of children the woman has borne. This may be due not only to varying lengths of exposure to the risk of childbearing, but also to changes in family size preferences that have taken place over time. Data are presented in Table 7.13 below.

As is evident from the data in Table 7.14, variations in family size preferences are clearly related to the number of children ever born to the women in this sample. Whether because of rationalization or actual targeting, the association is both linear and positive (p=.000; r=.347).

Also considered to be important in predicting overall fertility is the age at which women marry. Women who marry later are often thought to be less "traditional" than women who marry early, and women who marry later are exposed for shorter periods of time to the risk of childbearing. Since pre-marital sexual activity is not condoned in rural Java, the age at

TABLE 7.12: MEAN CHILDREN EVER BORN BY EDUCATION OF HUSBAND AND WIFE

Husband's Years of Schooling	CEB	Wife's Years of Schooling	CEB
0	5.0	0	4.9
1-3	4.8	1-3	4.2
4-6	3.5	4-6	3.6
7+	3.8	7+	3.5
Number of cases	394		394

Overall mean=4.1; both associations significantly linear: .000. Correlations = -.141 and -.177 respectively (Full sample). Correlations = -.122 and -.152 (Restricted sample)

TABLE 7.13:   CHILDREN EVER BORN BY MARITAL DURATION

Duration of Current Marriage	0	1-2	3-4	5-6	7+	Row %
< 6 years	25.0	75.0	0.0	0.0	0.0	100.0
6-10 years	2.9	65.7	24.3	4.3	2.9	100.0
11-15 years	4.5	24.7	58.4	9.0	3.4	100.0
16-20 years	0.0	8.5	52.5	27.1	11.9	100.0
21-25 years	5.6	3.7	22.2	40.7	27.8	100.0
26+ years	0.0	6.4	10.6	25.5	57.4	100.0

Chi-square=322.56;   d.f.=20;   significance level=.000.

TABLE 7.14:   CHILDREN EVER BORN BY IDEAL NUMBER OF CHILDREN

Ideal Number of Children Ever Born	0	1-2	3-4	5-6	7+	Row %
1-2	10.0	52.9	21.4	7.1	8.6	100.0
3-4	3.3	21.8	36.5	17.7	20.7	100.0
5-6	0.0	5.4	16.2	54.1	24.3	100.0
7+	0.0	25.0	12.5	0.0	62.5	100.0

Chi-square=322.56;   d.f.=20;   significance level=.000.

first marriage should be a particularly good predictor of fertility in that setting.

Bivariate tests of association demonstrate that that is, in fact, the case (Table 7.15). The relationship between fertility and age at first marriage is significant and linear. Women who married later were found to have had fewer children than were those who had married earlier and vice versa ($p=.000$; $r=-.194$). The average age at marriage among women who had had one or two children was 18.8, while the average age at marriage of those with seven or more children was considerably less, 15.7.

MULTIVARIATE DETERMINANTS OF CHILDREN EVER BORN

When the variable measuring children ever born is regressed on the independent variables in a standard OLS regression, most of the results are as anticipated (Table 7.16). For example, larger family size preferences and lengthier marital durations are clearly associated with higher fertility among the women in this sample. These effects are strong and significant in all equations in which they are introduced.

Duration of marriage is a good predictor of children ever born for a number of reasons, some of which have already been discussed. Those married longest ago tend to be the oldest and most traditional women, and those least exposed to western values or to non-traditional influences in general. In addition, they have also been exposed for the longest period of

TABLE 7.15:   WIFE'S MEAN AGE AT MARRIAGE BY CHILDREN EVER BORN

Number of Children Ever Born	Mean Age at Marriage
0	18.6
1-2	18.8
3-4	17.9
5-6	17.4
7+	15.7
Overall mean	17.6

TABLE 7.16: MULTIVARIATE DETERMINANTS OF CHILDREN EVER
BORN (Unstandardized Coefficients)

Independent Variable Equation:	1	2	3
Wife's decision-making power	-.056	.038	.054
Ideal family size	n.a.	.241***	.319 ***
Wife's education	.060	.047	.012
Husband's education	.060*	.053	.041
Wife's income (logged)	-.066	-.031	.010
Contraception (1=use, 0=no use)	n.a.	n.a.	1.047***
Marriage variables:			
Age at marriage	.006	.006	.022
Union order	.435	.378	.255
Duration of marriage	.222***	.209***	.215***
Constant	-.168	-1.096	-2.503
R Square	.53	.55	.58
Number of cases	293	292	291

* Significant at the .10 level; ** Significant at the
.05 level; ***Significant at the .01 level. Two-tailed
test of significance.

time to the risk of pregnancy.[9] Women who were married over 25 years prior to the survey were least affected by the government's efforts to bring about reductions in fertility, and many may have even completed their childbearing before information about contraception and family planning services became available in the villages.

The ever-use of contraception is also a significant predictor of fertility, but the direction of the effect is opposite to that anticipated.[10] In this case, contraceptive use is strongly and positively associated with the number of children ever born. While promoters of family planning programs generally operate under the assumption that increased access to and use of birth control methods will lead to declining fertility levels, the causation may at times run in the reverse direction. That appears to be the case among the couples in this sample, as contraception is often adopted in order to limit fertility after several children have already been born. In this research, being a contraceptive user is associated with having had approximately one child more, on average, than is true among non-users. Because the temporal order may be the opposite of that predicted, contraceptive use or non-use is probably a better predictor of whether or not an additional child will be conceived than of the number of children already born to the sampled women.

The only other variable that significantly influences fertility is the husband's education, and it is significant only when ideal family size and contraceptive use are not controlled. While higher education is frequently found to have a dampening effect on fertility in developing countries, that effect is often indirect. For example, increases in women's education tend to exert upward pressure on the age at first marriage, which, in turn, exerts downward pressure on fertility. When variables such as age at marriage are controlled, the effect of education frequently disappears, or in some cases, reverses.

There are several reasons why such a reversal can occur, particularly if it is the coefficient for the woman's education that becomes positive. In many parts of the world education still enhances a woman's "ability to have live births, probably through improved health, better nutrition, and the abandoning of traditional patterns of lactation and postpartum abstinence" (Cochrane, 1979:10). In addition, higher levels of education are often associated with more stable unions (and therefore with increased marital durations), and ultimately with increased exposure to the risk of pregnancy (Ware, 1981).

The fact that it is the husband's level of schooling that significantly affects fertility in this analysis, is probably as much related to the level of union stability as it is to any of the other factors described above. In addition, however, men from the upper socioeconomic strata are less likely than others to be constrained by the "Malthusian pressures" that have been argued to influence Indonesian contraception and fertility patterns.

All of the other variables included in this portion of the analysis were found to be non-significant in all three regressions estimated. The woman's age at marriage, her union order, and her education and income all fail to predict the number of children she has had when the other variables are controlled. More important for this particular analysis, however, is the fact that the variable measuring the woman's decision-making power remains non-significant in every estimation. As a result, Hypothesis 7.2 is not supported.

As has been mentioned, this may be due in part to the influence of the government's family planning program. Government officials appear eager to recruit new acceptors of all childbearing ages and backgrounds, yet as long as large families remain desirable in Java, women with the least power to resist outside pressures (be they social or economic), will generally be the ones most easily persuaded to join the program.

SUMMARY

Although the variables measuring parental contact and post-marriage mobility were expected to affect contraception and fertility only indirectly via their effects on the woman's decision-making power within the family, the mobility variables were found to have separate direct effects on the couple's contraceptive use or non-use. Compared to cases in which neither spouse moved after marriage, if either or both relocated, the likelihood that they had ever used contraception increased. The frequency with which couples discussed family planning matters also positively affected contraceptive use, as did being part of a more recent marriage cohort.

Variables that were found to exert a dampening influence upon contraception include the woman's desire to continue childbearing, membership in an earlier marriage cohort, the log value of the wife's income, and the amount of decision-making power she perceives herself to have within the household. Again, the latter was not anticipated, but probably reflects the fact that low-income women and those with very little control over household decisions might be the ones most susceptible to outside pressure to adopt contraception. The only variables not found to be significant predictors of contraception include the educational attainment levels of both spouses and the size of the community in which the wife lived prior to marriage.

As a consequence, neither hypothesis pertaining to contraceptive use is supported by the multivariate analysis. The evidence suggests that women with higher status both within and between households are less likely to use contraception than are women with lower status on both dimensions. Whereas the amount of discussion that takes place about contraception and other household matters can often be a good indicator of the level of equality within a relationship, in this case it may simply reflect the fact that before contraception is initiated a certain amount of discussion on the subject is likely to occur. Education is a good predictor of status across but not within categories of the other variables.

Three OLS regression equations were estimated to analyze fertility in rural Java. In the first equation, marital duration and the husband's level of schooling were both found to have a positive impact upon fertility. When the variable measuring ideal family size was added in the second equation, it too was found to exert a positive influence on CEB. The addition of that variable caused the coefficient measuring the husband's education to weaken and become non-significant, however.

In the final equation, the variable measuring contraceptive use was added. The effects of ideal family size and marital duration remained significant and positive, thus reaffirming that both lengthy marital unions and large family size preferences are associated with high levels of fertility. Not anticipated, however, was that the ever-use of contraception would also exert a positive effect upon fertility. This was argued to be a function of reverse causality, as women who had already had several children eventually decided to adopt contraception in order to limit further births.

Again, neither hypothesis pertaining to the impact of women's status upon fertility was supported. Although the bivariate association between education and fertility was significant and in the direction predicted, neither education variable was significant when all other variables were controlled.

NOTES

1. Data not presented.

2. In some cases it became apparent during the survey that "ideal" meant different things to different women, however. For example, a woman with two children might want three, state that three is ideal, and claim to want one more. Another woman, also with two children, might claim (1) that two are ideal, (2) that she does not want to stop childbearing, and (3) that she would like to have two more. It therefore appears as though the publicized ideals of the family planning programs are occasionally cited as ideal by women when their own preferences do not mesh with the official line.

3. The mobility variables are not divided by mobility before and after four years of marriage as they were in the chapter on decision-making power within marriage. It was expected that the timing of the move would be relatively unimportant in determining whether or not contraception was used, and that was found to be the case in preliminary analyses.

4. Refer to Chapter 6 for a review of the mobility patterns that characterize the couples in this sample.

5. (1) A 1 indicates that some form of birth control was utilized, while a 0 indicates that no use took place. (2) The variables introduced in this equation were found to explain 34 percent of the variance when a preliminary OLS regression was estimated.

6. In this analysis, care must be taken in making too much of the association between income and contraception, however. Current income is utilized as a predictor of completed childbearing, a process that may have taken place several years earlier. Although current income is used as a proxy for previous earnings, the causality may run in either direction.

7. Data not presented.

8. Since this part of the analysis is restricted to women who earned a cash income in the year preceding the survey, 25 percent of the original cases have been excluded. They were not replaced using the method of mean substitution because that procedure would have required that we assume that women who earn no income have roughly average levels of decision-making power. Much of the information discussed thus far has suggested that that is probably not the case.

9. Union order is controlled.

10. And it is clearly opposite to the one intended by government planners.

8

Summary and Conclusions

This research was designed to analyze the decision-making processes that take place within and between generations in four villages in rural Central Java. In addition, an attempt has been made to determine whether or not, and if so to what extent, variations in women's power to control decisions within the household influence specific demographic outcomes, in this case contraceptive use and overall fertility.

The first set of analyses explored the intergenerational dynamics involved in the process of mate selection. Recent research has suggested that shifts in the balance of decision-making power have been taking place throughout much of the world. Those getting married have gained strength in the decision-making process, while their parents' control has begun to diminish. In Chapter 5 an attempt was made to add to the existing, albeit limited body of literature on this topic by examining some of the determinants of the relative shifts in power between generations in Java.

From available information on familial transitions in the developing world in general, and in Indonesia in particular, several hypotheses were generated. To varying degrees, all have been supported. For example, it was posited that higher levels of education among the parents of the respondents should be associated with greater input into the marriage decision on the part of the respondents themselves. The data presented in Chapter 5 clearly demonstrate that that is the case. Whether husbands' or wives' perceptions of the decision-making process are studied separately, or whether their responses are pooled, the results consistently show that individual control over the process of mate selection does increase with the educational attainment levels of both fathers.

Although it was expected that higher levels of education among the respondents themselves would also enhance their ability to influence the marriage decision, much less uniform support was found for that hypothesis. Educational attainment was found to be of some importance among women, but only until duration of marriage was controlled. Once the variable measuring the length of the current union was included in the estimation, the effect of the woman's education was found to weaken and become non-significant.

This may have been in part because the marital duration variable was also measuring other factors associated with change over time, such as elements of socioeconomic development or changes in values and attitudes, that were not measured in this analysis. If that is the case, however, those changes must all have taken place net of the educational advances experienced by both generations, net of increasing ages at marriage, and net of the size of the community in which the woman lived before her wedding.

Among the male respondents, higher education was not found to have significantly increased their input into the decision to marry. When the data on the two spouses were pooled, the effect of schooling among the women was powerful enough to sustain a significant coefficient, but again only until marital duration was controlled.

An attempt was then made to ascertain whether or not increased schooling might have been of disproportionate benefit to women in the decision-making process, and that was found to be the case. Additional increments of education improved the decision-making power of women (relative to their parents) in making the marriage decision, more than they did for the men. This was probably because until recently, extended school attendance was far more common among males than among females.

It was expected that the size of the community in which the respondent lived prior to marriage should play a major role in influencing the balance of decision-making power between generations. Increases in both education and urban exposure have often been argued to increase access to more modern (or western) ideas, such as those promoting family nucleation and increasing rights for women, both within the family and across society. As predicted, it was found that women who lived in large urban centers before marriage exercised much greater control over the marriage decision than did women who came from smaller urban or rural areas.

Pre-marital urban residence was much less important for males, however. That may be because they had completed more years of schooling on average than had their wives, and thus had gained exposure to outside influences through several channels, or it may be because relatively few males had lived in a large urban center prior to their marriage. When the data on husbands and wives were pooled, the effect of size of pre-marital residence was not found to be significant, even when marital duration was not controlled.

It was hypothesized that those who married at older ages would report having had more input into the marriage decision than would those who were married at younger ages. Among the husbands, this was found to be the case. Among the women, however, age at marriage significantly affected their decision-making power only when marital duration was not controlled. For them, age at marriage was therefore salient to the intergenerational dynamic across, but not within levels of marital duration.

Respondents in higher order unions were expected to have had more control over the decisions surrounding their current marriages than were individuals still reporting on a first marriage. Although union order did not successfully affect the decision-making power of the male respondents, the results among women were generally as predicted. When age at marriage was not controlled, women still in their first marriages had much less to say about whom they would marry than was true for women in higher-order unions. When age at marriage was controlled, however, the coefficient for union order became non-significant.

The hypothesis focusing on the importance of union order was generated on the basis of the background material presented in Chapter 3. It suggested that although individuals in Indonesia still tend to honor the wishes of their parents when deciding whom to marry the first time, it is not uncommon for them to get divorced and remarried, the next time to someone of their own choosing. It is interesting to note that as individual input into the marriage decision has begun to increase, divorce rates in much of the country have begun to decline.

As is true throughout much of the demographic literature, the importance of change over time has been a recurring theme throughout this analysis. Net of temporal changes associated with the variables that have already been discussed, it was hypothesized that individuals married longer ago would report having faced more severe parental constraints in choosing a spouse than would those married more recently. In all estimations run for both male and female respondents that hypothesis received strong support. Even given controls for the educational attainment levels of both the respondents and their fathers, the ages at marriage of both spouses, and the size of each respondent's community of residence prior to marriage, the marital duration variable was strong and significant.

Given the strength of that variable, it was thought that the impact of change over time on the dynamics involved in the marriage decision warranted further investigation. As a result, the female sample was split by length of marital duration, separating those married for fewer than 15 years from those married for 15 years or more. The results indicate that both the educational attainment of the respondents themselves and the level of schooling of their fathers played much greater roles in improving the decision-making power of women married within 15 years of the survey than they did for women married longer ago. The same was true of the variable measuring marital duration itself. Not only advances in education, but also change over time that is independent of the other predictor variables, have therefore had a greater impact upon women's status in recent years than was true earlier on.

Why recent increases in respondents' education have been especially important to the decision-making process is fairly easily explained, although why that is also the case for their fathers' education is less certain. The fact that the social climate has only recently become ripe for variation in the decision-making dynamic by level of fathers' schooling is probably related to the timing of earlier advances in education for men, however.

Unlike education and marital duration, the size of the community in which the respondent lived before marriage was found to be particularly salient to the decision-making power of women who had been married 15 or more years before the survey. This was argued to be due, at least in part, to the fact that recent improvements in transportation and increases in commuting throughout Java have combined to make premarital residence in a city much less important than it once was as a means by which exposure to modern or western values could be acquired.

Age at marriage was also found to be a better predictor of decision-making power among older than among younger cohorts. That is probably because women who were married longer ago were much more apt to have married very early, sometimes when they were little more than children, than were women who were married more recently. As the average age at first marriage increased among the early cohorts, so did the likelihood that those getting married would be allowed at least some input into the decision-making process.

Given the results of the analyses discussed so far, it was also thought that, net of other factors, change over time might have been of disproportionate benefit to women in the decision-making process. Unlike the coefficient gauging the interaction between gender and education, however, the coefficient measuring the interaction between gender and marital duration was not significant. The data thus suggest that change over time as measured by marital duration has not been of particular benefit to women compared to men in the process of mate selection in Java.

On the other hand, as long as age at marriage was not controlled, men did report having had more input into the marriage decision than did their wives. (Gender and age at marriage were highly correlated). Without that control, and with the inclusion of the variables measuring the interactions of gender with level of education and marital duration, women's decision-making scores were found to be lower than those of their husbands by 51 percentage points. This was important not only within the context of the dynamics involved in the marriage decision, but also because it set the stage for the second section of the analysis.

As a rule, once the decisions leading up to a marriage have been made in Indonesia, the intergenerational component does not disappear from the decision-making process. Instead, spouses become central to the dynamic, while parents retain at least a peripheral interest in decision outcomes. The second portion of this research was designed to examine some of the intricacies of the decision-making processes that occur once a couple has married.

The central hypotheses in the second analysis chapter focused primarily on post-nuptial migration and the frequency with which contact was maintained with the parents on both sides of the family. Again, all gained at least partial support. First, it was predicted that a move that allowed the couple to establish a degree of independence from parents and extended kin would enhance the woman's decision-making power within the family, and that this would be particularly relevant if the move took place within the first four years of the couple's marriage. Compared to cases in which neither the husband nor the wife had as yet moved, and compared to situations in which only one spouse had changed her/his place of residence, a post-marriage move made by both spouses within the first four years of marriage was expected to increase the level of control the woman had over household decisions.

The data suggest that that is the case. When neither spouse moved within the first four years of their union, or when only the husband moved, the wife was found to have considerably less to say in decisions about the initiation of contraception than was true when both she and her husband relocated. In addition, when the woman's overall decision-making power was estimated, her intra-household status was found to be lower in cases in which neither spouse moved than when they both relocated within the first four years.

It was also expected that, compared to cases in which both spouses moved after four years of marriage, women in the reference group (in which both spouses moved within the first four years) would have greater overall decision-making power. It was thought that couples who established their own homes comparatively early in the marriage would develop especially egalitarian relationships. That was not found to be the case, however. The status of women in the reference category was not significantly different from that of women who made a joint move with their husbands later in the marriage.

Although the timing of the move was not initially found to be important in and of itself, an attempt was also made to gauge the salience of the distance covered by the move and the relationship between timing and distance. It was predicted that if the couple's relocation required that the woman move beyond the borders of her village, her intra-household status would suffer compared to that of women who did not make an exogamous move. That hypothesis was generated on the basis of information that suggested that the benefits of post-nuptial migration could easily be overridden by the disadvantages associated with the disruption of the woman's social networks.

As expected, it was found that exogamous relocation early in a marriage did indeed reduce the decision-making power of the women in this sample. The effect was significant in the estimation of power in the contraception decision, as well as in that measuring control over the decision to limit further childbearing. If, however, the inter-village relocation took place after the couple had been married for at least four years, the wife's decision-making power was then found to improve. At that point the importance of her support systems apparently diminished, while the establishment of an independent residence became especially salient to the decision-making process. Together these findings demonstrate that, depending upon both the distance and the timing of a post-nuptial move, women can gain considerable influence within the household through residential relocation.

Finally, it was predicted that women in marriages in which frequent contact is maintained with either or both sets of parents should have lower intra-household status than should women in marriages in which frequent contact is not maintained with the parents on either side of the family. Support was also attained for that hypothesis. When parents on both sides of the family were seen on a regular basis, the wife's intra-familial status suffered notably compared to cases in which no regular contact was reported. That was found to be the case in the estimation of the woman's overall decision-making power, as well as in the analyses pertaining to future childbearing and the allocation of the wife's earnings.

Because residential mobility remained a significant predictor even when the level of parental contact was controlled, it is evident that the actual physical relocation of the couple can have an independent effect upon the decision-making power of women in rural Java. Conversely, regardless of whether or not a move takes place, the amount of contact that is maintained with the parents on both spouses can have a significant impact upon the decision-making process.

As has been discussed, several levels of participation are likely to be involved in each of these decisions. While parents do not necessarily have direct input into the decisions, they certainly help to mold the contexts in which the decisions are made. This appears to be particularly important in cases in which sons and daughters continue to co-reside with their parents or to see them a number of times each week.

The salience of intergenerational dynamics to the decision-making process was reaffirmed in this analysis, as previous input into the marriage decision was found to be significant and positive in four of the five equations estimated in Chapter 6. The more input both women and men had in the decision to marry, the more control they were then able to exercise in later household decisions.

The impact of the independent variables measuring education and income on the woman's decision-making power differed with the analysis being conducted. The indicator for the wife's own earnings had an effect on her overall decision-making power and on her input into the decision to stop having children, while the level of her husband's income affected her ability to govern the use of her own earnings. As a rule, however, once the other variables were controlled, the education variables were found to be of little importance in affecting a woman's ability to influence the decision-making process; only the husband's educational attainment proved to be significant in predicting her overall decision-making power.

While neither education variable significantly affected the husband's ability to control household decisions, the levels of both his own income and that of his wife were found to influence his overall decision-making power. The more he earned, the more he had to say about household matters, while the more she earned, the less control he was able to exert in the process. This was argued to reflect the importance for women of access to resources in determining their power in household negotiations. With less access, their relative power within the household (and probably the broader community as well) often becomes very limited.

Finally, the impact of the variable measuring duration of marriage was somewhat ambiguous. While it failed to predict any of the dependent variables gauging women's decision-making power, the length of time spent in the current union was found to significantly affect males' perceptions of their inputs into the decision-making process. The longer the couple had been married, the more control the husband felt he had over important household matters. Given the controls for parental contact, this suggests that women who were married more recently should have more to say vis-a-vis their husbands, than should those married longer ago. Inter-spousal relationships in rural portions of Central Java may therefore be becoming increasingly egalitarian as the intra-household status of women in the region improves.

This must remain a hypothesis for the time being, however, since the complete experience of the younger cohorts cannot yet be assessed. Future research will have to take a more in-depth look at these issues if more definitive information about that element of the decision-making process is to be ascertained.

Despite the fact that little substantive evidence was previously available on the specific topics investigated in Chapters 5 and 6, at least some support was offered for every hypothesis tested. Although the issues addressed in Chapter 7 have been much more commonly researched, the hypotheses introduced in that chapter have proved to be much less successful in predicting the outcomes of interest. That portion of the analysis focused on the degree to which the status of women, both within the household and to a lesser extent throughout the broader community, affects contraceptive use and overall fertility.

It was predicted that women with high levels of intra-household status would be the ones most likely to have ever used some form of contraception. Instead, the opposite was found to be true among the women in this sample. It was argued that given the sometimes coercive nature of Indonesia's family planning program, women with more power to control decisions within the household might also be those best able to resist outside pressures to adopt contraception when it is not desired. Whereas female decision-making power and ideal family size were inversely correlated, once family size was controlled the women with more strength to control matters within the household were found to be less likely than other women to have ever used contraception.

This may help explain why women at the bottom of the earnings scale are so much more likely than those in the middle tiers to use contraception. Although it was anticipated in this analysis that increases in extra-household status, as measured by variables such as income and education, would also increase the likelihood that the couple would have used contraception at some point during their marriage, that was not found to be the case either.

The educational attainment levels of both spouses were found to be significantly and positively associated with contraceptive use, but only at the bivariate level. When other variables that are highly related to education, such as the desire for additional children and the frequency with which contraception is discussed in the home, were controlled, the education coefficients became nonsignificant. In addition, the coefficient for the wife's earnings was significant and negative in this analysis. The related hypothesis therefore was not supported, as women with lower status on the second dimension were also found to be less likely to have ever used contraception than were higher status women.

When the determinants of the number of children ever born were examined, the dependent variable was found to vary predictably with the measures of ideal family size and marital duration. In the most simple model estimated, increases in the levels of the husbands' education were also found to exert a positive effect on parity. Perhaps the most interesting finding, however, was that being an ever-user of contraception had a strong positive association with fertility as well. That result was not anticipated. Because it is not clear at what point in the parity progression contraceptive use actually occurred, however, the causal ordering of the variables measuring contraception and fertility is assumed to be backwards. Contraception was most likely being used as a means to discontinue childbearing by those who had had all the children they desired, while low parity women who had not yet reached their fertility targets had not yet used any method of birth control.

IMPLICATIONS

What do these findings suggest? First, young men and women in Indonesia are increasingly able to control decisions concerning whom they will marry. As arranged marriages become less and less common, divorce rates may continue to decline as well, at least for the time being.

Second, it is clear that the Javanese woman's ability to influence household decisions generally improves when both spouses change their place of residence within the first four years of marriage; that is, unless the move is an exogamous one. If, however, the move requires inter-village relocation on the part of the wife early in the marriage, her power to control matters within the household instead diminishes. Related to this is the fact that under certain circumstances more frequent contact with the parents of both spouses reduces the woman's power to influence household decisions. Women's autonomy within the family may thus increase as variations in parental contact and residential mobility patterns continue to evolve. Postnuptial migration that allows the couple greater independence from parental supervision without isolating the woman from important social networks early in her married life should improve her ability to affect the outcomes of important household decisions.

As Java becomes more and more crowded, however, options regarding post-marriage mobility may become increasingly limited. Couples may have to live with in-laws for longer periods of time, and they may have to move farther away from social networks when establishing new households. Extended co-residence with either set of parents is likely to continue to restrict the wife's input into household decisions, as is migration to a distant village early in the marriage. If the problem of land scarcity becomes particularly acute, the early establishment of independent households within selected villages may become less and less feasible.

Improvements in the status of women are nevertheless likely to continue to occur in Indonesia via such mechanisms as increases in education and employment opportunities. The current government has been committed for some time to raising women's status through these and other avenues, although one of the primary rationales behind such policies has been that improvements in the social position of women should produce increases in contraceptive use and decreases in fertility. The results of this analysis suggest, however, that the linkages between women's status, contraception and fertility are not always those anticipated. For example, at the time of our survey relatively large families remained attractive to many Indonesian women, and the higher status women we interviewed appeared to be those who had been best able to resist program pressure to adopt contraception.

As a result, it appears as though there now exists at least an underlying adversarial relationship between the stated goals of the family planning program and the reproductive targets of a number of women in Javanese society. Changes in contraceptive behavior are at times brought about only after a certain amount of pressure has been exerted on the acceptor, since personal values and policy objectives do not always coincide. Thus far, it has been the women with comparatively high autonomy who have been best able to resist program influence when the latter is contrary to their own preferences.

On the other hand, despite the fact that increases in the intra-and extra-household status of women are not always immediately effective in limiting fertility, it is likely that they will eventually play an important role in that regard and thus should be encouraged. Women with high intra-household status have lower ideal family sizes than do women with less power within the home; they tend to marry later, and they are characterized by comparatively high levels of extrahousehold status as well.

Because continued fertility reduction is desired by the government, one immediate priority should be to further reduce family size preferences, a factor that is clearly recognized by policy makers in Indonesia as crucial to the eventual success of their program, rather than to encourage couples to adopt a strategy for which they may not otherwise be ready. Once couples establish lower reproductive targets, it is likely that the higher status women will be among those with the lowest fertility.

Appendix

	MARDUR	AGEMAR	WIFEINC	HUSB.INC
MARDUR	1.0000	-.3675**	.1121	-.0108
AGEMAR	-.3675**	1.0000	.0559	.1123
WIFEINC	.1121	.0559	1.0000	.2363**
HUSB.INC	-.0108	.1123	.2363**	1.0000
HUSB.EDUC	-.3639**	.1430*	.3027**	.4513**
WIFE EDUC	-.4039**	.1987**	.2900**	.3527**
V24	-.3173**	.2159**	.0048	.0280
M24	-.2154**	.2227**	-.0415	.0350
V41	.4470**	-.0454	.0923	.1615**
V46	-.1869**	-.0373	-.0225	.0963
V66	.0283	-.0331	.2836**	-.0177
ZDEC	.2353**	-.1065	.1720**	.1128
MZDEC	.2757**	-.0825	.0275	.0954
M41	.4573**	-.0438	.0462	.0140
M46	-.1374*	-.0487	.0236	.1463*
M66	.0116	-.0108	-.0442	.0200
M33	-.3978**	-.0399	-.0990	-.0451
V33	-.3580**	-.0064	-.0560	.1379*
BOTHREG	-.3444**	-.0066	-.0543	.0670
WIFEPREG	.0492	-.0121	.0750	.0616
HUSPREG	-.0862	.0282	-.0317	-.1091
NOREG	.3668**	-.0082	.0108	-.0223
BOTHMOV4	.0988	-.0510	.0338	.1269*
BOTHMOVE	-.1049	.0540	.0265	.0435
WIFEMOVE	.0274	-.0391	.0272	-.0285
HUSBMOVE	.0014	-.0481	-.0853	-.1024
NOMOVE	.0340	.0769	.0072	.0191
MOVEVILL	-.1015	.0840	.0138	.0059
MOVEVIL4	.0107	.0286	.0701	.0124
V21	.0668	-.0338	.0357	.0204
V16	.0799	.2432**	.0267	.0327
FATHED	-.2875**	.0901	.1489*	.1692**
HFATHED	-.2062**	.1164	.1338*	.2456**

	HUSB.EDUC.	WIFE EDUC.	V66	ZDEC
MARDUR	-.3639**	-.4039**	.0283	.2353**
AGEMAR	.1430*	.1987**	-.0331	-.1065
WIFEINC	.3027**	.2900**	.2836**	.1720**
HUSB.INC	.4513**	.3527**	-.0177	.1128
HUSB.EDUC	1.0000	.6871**	.0292	.0781
WIFE EDUC	.6871**	1.0000	.1010	.0750
V24	.2531**	.2999**	-.0733	.0071
M24	.1159	.1885**	-.1349*	-.0285
V41	-.0687	-.0962	.0385	.5793**
V46	.2534**	.2936**	-.0015	.4957**
V66	.0292	.1010	1.0000	.4537**
ZDEC	.0781	.0750	.4537**	1.0000
MZDEC	.0051	.0032	-.0606	.5014**
M41	-.1642**	-.1629**	-.0296	.4329**
M46	.2553**	.2542**	-.0625	.3886**
M66	-.0059	-.0075	-.0168	.0039
M33	.1390*	.1211*	.0140	-.1093
V33	.2293**	.1789**	-.0359	-.0752
BOTHREG	.1782**	.1303*	-.0325	-.1715**
WIFEPREG	.0411	.0706	-.0184	.1121
HUSPREG	.0054	.0100	.0826	.0285
NOREG	-.2166**	-.2025**	-.0275	.0336
BOTHMOV4	.0709	.0154	.0278	.0616
BOTHMOVE	.0248	.1394*	-.0562	.0447
WIFEMOVE	-.0728	-.0636	.0377	-.0171
HUSBMOVE	-.0353	-.0235	.0115	-.0120
NOMOVE	.0636	-.0825	-.0102	-.0653
MOVEVILL	.0364	.0528	-.0575	-.0324
MOVEVIL4	.0466	.0022	.0497	.0762
V21	-.0545	-.0922	.0824	-.0628
V16	-.1114	-.1977**	-.0404	-.0036
FATHED	.4604**	.6061**	.0320	.0040
HFATHED	.5378**	.4474**	-.0146	.0328

	V24	M24	V41	V46
MARDUR	-.3173**	-.2154**	.4470**	-.1869**
AGEMAR	.2159**	.2227**	-.0454	-.0373
WIFEINC	.0048	-.0415	.0923	-.0225
HUSB.INC	.0280	.0350	.1615**	.0963
HUSB.EDUC	.2531**	.1159	-.0687	.2534**
WIFE EDUC	.2999**	.1885**	-.0962	.2936**
V24	1.0000	.5852**	.0032	.1384*
M24	.5852**	1.0000	.0299	.1205
V41	.0032	.0299	1.0000	.2033**
V46	.1384*	.1205	.2033**	1.0000
V66	-.0733	-.1349*	.0385	-.0015
ZDEC	.0071	-.0285	.5793**	.4957**
MZDEC	.0482	.1686**	.5272**	.4462**
M41	-.0321	.0727	.6936**	.1887**
M46	.0902	.1221*	.2138**	.6964**
M66	.1221*	.2278**	.1000	.0233
M33	.0585	-.0049	-.2829**	.1091
V33	.0677	.1060	-.1964**	.1168
BOTHREG	.0635	.0154	-.2258**	.0360
WIFEPREG	.0310	.0682	.0882	.0437
HUSPREG	-.0398	-.0495	-.0589	.0410
NOREG	-.0541	-.0338	.1896**	-.1142
BOTHMOV4	-.0677	-.0531	.0898	.0525
BOTHMOVE	.1165	.1118	.0285	.0780
WIFEMOVE	-.0959	-.1180	-.0364	.0212
HUSBMOVE	-.0375	.0122	-.0294	-.0131
NOMOVE	.0704	.0363	-.0138	-.1576*
MOVEVILL	.0358	.0524	-.1064	.0563
MOVEVIL4	-.0102	-.0040	.1336*	.0259
V21	-.1292*	-.0672	-.0468	-.1183
V16	.0482	.0990	.0891	-.1189
FATHED	.2907**	.1868**	-.0841	.2000**
HFATHED	.2174**	.1677**	-.0653	.1379*

	MZDEC	M41	M46	M66
MARDUR	.2757**	.4573**	-.1374*	.0116
AGEMAR	-.0825	-.0438	-.0487	-.0108
WIFEINC	.0275	.0462	.0236	-.0442
HUSB.INC	.0954	.0140	.1463*	.0200
HUSB.EDUC	.0051	-.1642**	.2553**	-.0059
WIFE EDUC	.0032	-.1629**	.2542**	-.0075
V24	.0482	-.0321	.0902	.1221*
M24	.1686**	.0727	.1221*	.2278**
V41	.5272**	.6936**	.2138**	.1000
V46	.4462**	.1887**	.6964**	.0233
V66	-.0606	-.0296	-.0625	-.0168
ZDEC	.5014**	.4329**	.3886**	.0039
MZDEC	1.0000	.7150**	.6151**	.4792**
M41	.7150**	1.0000	.2719**	.0973
M46	.6151**	.2719**	1.0000	.0613
M66	.4792**	.0973	.0613	1.0000
M33	-.1168	-.2438**	.0863	-.0133
V33	-.0879	-.1909**	.1023	.0393
BOTHREG	-.1483*	-.2130**	.0246	-.0258
WIFEPREG	.0665	.0768	.0219	.0384
HUSPREG	-.0007	-.0297	.0558	-.0321
NOREG	.0814	.1611**	-.0962	.0184
BOTHMOV4	.0906	.1042	.0797	-.0047
BOTHMOVE	-.0199	.0092	.0359	-.0464
WIFEMOVE	.0156	-.0084	.0187	-.0074
HUSBMOVE	.0219	-.0085	-.0123	.0057
NOMOVE	-.0855	-.0632	-.1164	.0703
MOVEVILL	-.0108	-.0230	.0646	-.0347
MOVEVIL4	.0283	.0840	.0067	.0120
V21	-.0767	-.0033	-.0418	-.1695**
V16	.0287	.1647**	-.0615	-.0840
FATHED	-.0167	-.1020	.1705**	-.0314
HFATHED	-.0139	-.1497*	.0681	.0286

	M33	V33	BOTHMOV4	BOTHMOVE
MARDUR	-.3978**	-.3580**	.0988	-.1049
AGEMAR	-.0399	-.0064	-.0510	.0540
WIFEINC	-.0990	-.0560	.0338	.0265
HUSB.INC	-.0451	.1379*	.1269*	.0435
HUSB.EDUC	.1390*	.2293**	.0709	.0248
WIFE EDUC	.1211*	.1789**	.0154	.1394*
V24	.0585	.0677	-.0677	.1165
M24	-.0049	.1060	-.0531	.1118
V41	-.2829**	-.1964**	.0898	.0285
V46	.1091	.1168	.0525	.0780
V66	.0140	-.0359	.0278	-.0562
ZDEC	-.1093	-.0752	.0616	.0447
MZDEC	-.1168	-.0879	.0906	-.0199
M41	-.2438**	-.1909**	.1042	.0092
M46	.0863	.1023	.0797	.0359
M66	-.0133	.0393	-.0047	-.0464
M33	1.0000	.1228*	-.0305	.1405*
V33	.1228*	1.0000	-.0459	.0125
BOTHREG	.5168**	.4481**	-.0631	.0264
WIFEPREG	-.4078**	.4694**	-.0007	-.0050
HUSPREG	.4862**	-.3642**	.0088	.0908
NOREG	-.5640**	-.5421**	.0536	-.1048
BOTHMOV4	-.0305	-.0459	1.0000	-.1544*
BOTHMOVE	.1405*	.0125	-.1544*	1.0000
WIFEMOVE	-.0755	-.1771**	-.1688**	-.4356**
HUSBMOVE	-.0443	.1815**	-.1270*	-.3278**
NOMOVE	-.0090	.0411	-.0919	-.2371**
MOVEVILL	-.0024	-.1811**	-.1698**	.1338*
MOVEVIL4	-.0721	-.0476	.1531*	-.1153
V21	.0094	.0283	.0442	-.0948
V16	-.1959**	-.0819	.0253	-.0536
FATHED	.1143	.0639	-.0030	.1132
HFATHED	.1171	.0602	.0033	.0681

	BOTHREG	WIFEPREG	HUSPREG	NOREG
MARDUR	-.3444**	.0492	-.0862	.3668**
AGEMAR	-.0066	-.0121	.0282	-.0082
WIFEINC	-.0543	.0750	-.0317	.0108
HUSB.INC	.0670	.0616	-.1091	-.0223
HUSB.EDUC	.1782**	.0411	.0054	-.2166**
WIFE EDUC	.1303*	.0706	.0100	-.2025**
V24	.0635	.0310	-.0398	-.0541
M24	.0154	.0682	-.0495	-.0338
V41	-.2258**	.0882	-.0589	.1896**
V46	.0360	.0437	.0410	-.1142
V66	-.0325	-.0184	.0826	-.0275
ZDEC	-.1715**	.1121	.0285	.0336
MZDEC	-.1483*	.0665	-.0007	.0814
M41	-.2130**	.0768	-.0297	.1611**
M46	.0246	.0219	.0558	-.0962
M66	-.0258	.0384	-.0321	.0184
M33	.5168**	-.4078**	.4862**	-.5640**
V33	.4481**	.4694**	-.3642**	-.5421**
BOTHREG	1.0000	-.3284**	-.3138**	-.3672**
WIFEPREG	-.3284**	1.0000	-.3005**	-.3517**
HUSPREG	-.3138**	-.3005**	1.0000	-.3361**
NOREG	-.3672**	-.3517**	-.3361**	1.0000
BOTHMOV4	-.0631	-.0007	.0088	.0536
BOTHMOVE	.0264	-.0050	.0908	-.1048
WIFEMOVE	-.1272*	-.1444*	.0860	.1805**
HUSBMOVE	.1179	.1710**	-.2151**	-.0774
NOMOVE	.0422	-.0001	.0144	-.0541
MOVEVILL	-.2224**	-.1473*	.2206**	.1510*
MOVEVIL4	-.0023	-.0311	-.0613	.0883
V21	.0698	-.0460	-.0164	-.0089
V16	-.0951	.0763	-.1025	.1146
FATHED	.0392	-.0029	.0663	-.0966
HFATHED	.0438	-.0185	.0963	-.1140

	WIFEMOVE	HUSBMOVE	NOMOVE	MOVEVILL
MARDUR	.0274	.0014	.0340	-.1015
AGEMAR	-.0391	-.0481	.0769	.0840
WIFEINC	.0272	-.0853	.0072	.0138
HUSB.INC	-.0285	-.1024	.0191	.0059
HUSB.EDUC	-.0728	-.0353	.0636	.0364
WIFE EDUC	-.0636	-.0235	-.0825	.0528
V24	-.0959	-.0375	.0704	.0358
M24	-.1180	.0122	.0363	.0524
V41	-.0364	-.0294	-.0138	-.1064
V46	.0212	-.0131	-.1576*	.0563
V66	.0377	.0115	-.0102	-.0575
ZDEC	-.0171	-.0120	-.0653	-.0324
MZDEC	.0156	.0219	-.0855	-.0108
M41	-.0084	-.0085	-.0632	-.0230
M46	.0187	-.0123	-.1164	.0646
M66	-.0074	.0057	.0703	-.0347
M33	-.0755	-.0443	-.0090	-.0024
BOTHREG	-.1272*	.1179	.0422	-.2224**
WIFEPREG	-.1444*	.1710**	-.0001	-.1473*
HUSPREG	.0860	-.2151**	.0144	.2206**
NOREG	.1805**	-.0774	-.0541	.1510*
BOTHMOV4	-.1688**	-.1270*	-.0919	-.1698**
BOTHMOVE	-.4356**	-.3278**	-.2371**	.1338*
WIFEMOVE	1.0000	-.3583**	-.2592**	.4538**
HUSBMOVE	-.3583**	1.0000	-.1951**	-.3605**
NOMOVE	-.2592**	-.1951**	1.0000	-.2608**
MOVEVILL	.4538**	-.3605**	-.2608**	1.0000
MOVEVIL4	-.1260*	.1284*	.0701	-.1268*
V21	-.0098	.0362	.0679	-.1763**
V16	.0896	-.0384	-.0238	.0233
FATHED	.0377	-.0738	-.1150	.1842**
HFATHED	-.0196	-.0897	.0437	.1508*

	MOVEVIL4	V21	V16	FATHED	HFATHED
MARDUR	.0107	.0668	.0799	-.2875**	-.2062**
AGEMAR	.0286	-.0338	.2432**	.0901	.1164
WIFEINC	.0701	.0357	.0267	.1489*	.1338*
HUSB.INC	.0124	.0204	.0327	.1692**	.2456**
HUSB.EDUC	.0466	-.0545	-.1114	.4604**	.5378**
WIFE EDUC	.0022	-.0922	-.1977**	.6061**	.4474**
V24 .	-.0102	-.1292*	.0482	.2907**	.2174**
M24	-.0040	-.0672	.0990	.1868**	.1677**
V41	.1336*	-.0468	.0891	-.0841	-.0653
V46	.0259	-.1183	-.1189	.2000**	.1379*
V66	.0497	.0824	-.0404	.0320	-.0146
ZDEC	.0762	-.0628	-.0036	.0040	.0328
MZDEC	.0283	-.0767	.0287	-.0167	-.0139
M41	.0840	-.0033	.1647**	-.1020	-.1497*
M46	.0067	-.0418	-.0615	.1705**	.0681
M66	.0120	-.1695**	-.0840	-.0314	.0286
M33	-.0721	.0094	-.1959**	.1143	.1171
V33	-.0476	.0283	-.0819	.0639	.0602
BOTHREG	-.0023	.0698	-.0951	.0392	.0438
WIFEPREG	-.0311	-.0460	.0763	-.0029	-.0185
HUSPREG	-.0613	-.0164	-.1025	.0663	.0963
NOREG	.0883	-.0089	.1146	-.0966	-.1140
BOTHMOV4	.1531*	.0442	.0253	-.0030	.0033
BOTHMOVE	-.1153	-.0948	-.0536	.1132	.0681
WIFEMOVE	-.1260*	-.0098	.0896	.0377	-.0196
HUSBMOVE	.1284*	.0362	-.0384	-.0738	-.0897
NOMOVE	.0701	.0679	-.0238	-.1150	.0437
MOVEVILL	-.1268*	-.1763**	.0233	.1842**	.1508*
MOVEVIL4	1.0000	-.0559	.0491	.0207	.0684
V21	-.0559	1.0000	.0550	-.0273	-.1144
V16	.0491	.0550	1.0000	-.1678**	-.0441
FATHED	.0207	-.0273	-.1678**	1.0000	.4486**
HFATHED	.0684	-.1144	-.0441	.4486**	1.0000

Variables in Matrix:

Mardur = Duration of marriage
Agemar = Age at marriage
Wifeinc = Wife's income
Husb.inc = Husband's income
Husb. Educ = Husband's education
Wife Educ = Wife's education
V24 = Marriage decision (wife)
M24 = Marriage decision (husband)
V41 = Childbearing decision (wife)
V46 = Contraception decision (wife)
V66 = Resource control decision (wife)
Zdec = Standardized variable for wife's overall
    decision-making power
Mzdec = Standardized variable for husband's overall
    decision-making power
M41 = Childbearing decision (husband)
M46 = Contraception decision (husband)
M66 = Resource control decision (husband)
M33 = Frequency of visits with husband's mother
V33 = Frequency of visits with wife's mother
Bothreg = See parents on both sides regularly
Wifepreg = See wife's parents regularly
Husbpreg = See husband's parents regularly
Noreg = See neither set of parents regularly
Bothmov4 = Both moved more than 4 years after marriage
Bothmove = Both moved within 4 years of marriage
Wifemove = Wife moved
Husbmove = Husband moved
Nomove = Neither moved
Movevill = Inter-villiage move within 4 years of marriage
Movevil4 = Inter-villiage move more than 4 years after
    marriage
V21 = Type of pre-marital residence (wife)
V16 = First marriage or not (wife)
Fathed = Father's education (wife)
Hfathed = Father's education (husband)

VARIABLES USED IN CHAPTER 7

	V45	V44	V43	V38
V45	1.0000	.4110**	-.0616	-.1254
V44	.4110**	1.0000	-.1074	.0720
V43	-.0616	-.1074	1.0000	-.0874
V38	-.1254	.0720	-.0874	1.0000
V36	.0490	-.1416*	.3323**	-.5609**
V66	-.1323	-.0082	-.0415	-.0059
V8	.2774**	.3579**	.0009	.1258
M8	.2530**	.3215**	.0191	.0801
V64	-.0233	.0499	-.0461	-.1272
M64	.1221	.1399*	-.0099	-.0996
V21	-.0933	-.0445	.0754	-.0256
V16	-.0238	-.0903	.0682	-.1542*
AGEMAR	.0088	-.0224	-.0674	.0485
MARDUR	-.2149**	-.2408**	.2472**	-.5452**
BOTHMOVE	.0436	.0669	-.0222	-.0188
WIFEMOVE	.0642	.0614	.0772	-.0240
HUSBMOVE	.0031	-.0856	-.0603	.0420
LONGMAR	-.2791**	-.2833**	.2003**	-.3274**
SHORTMAR	.1984**	.2298**	-.1736*	.4785**

	V36	V66	V21	V16
V45	.0490	-.1323	-.0933	-.0238
V44	-.1416*	-.0082	-.0445	-.0903
V43	.3323**	-.0415	.0754	.0682
V38	-.5609**	-.0059	-.0256	-.1542*
V36	1.0000	.0195	.0835	.0792
V66	.0195	1.0000	-.0957	-.0102
V8	-.1521*	.0753	-.1054	-.1963**
M8	-.1219	.0174	-.0995	-.0896
V64	.0951	.0108	-.0033	.0209
M64	.0664	.1467*	.0503	-.0405
V21	.0835	-.0957	1.0000	.0230
V16	.0792	-.0102	.0230	1.0000
AGEMAR	-.2259**	-.0539	-.1244	.2652**
MARDUR	.7099**	.0413	.1198	.0473
BOTHMOVE	.0062	-.0193	-.0108	-.0776
WIFEMOVE	-.0170	.0675	-.0444	.0347
HUSBMOVE	.0354	-.0547	.0369	-.0075
LONGMAR	.4884**	.0404	.0742	-.0046
SHORTMAR	-.6135**	.0161	-.1069	-.0969

	V8	M8	V64	M64
V45	.2774**	.2530**	-.0233	.1221
V44	.3579**	.3215**	.0499	.1399*
V43	.0009	.0191	-.0461	-.0099
V38	.1258	.0801	-.1272	-.0996
V36	-.1521*	-.1219	.0951	.0664
V66	.0753	.0174	.0108	.1467*
V8	1.0000	.7255**	.3178**	.4157**
M8	.7255**	1.0000	.3585**	.4945**
V64	.3178**	.3585**	1.0000	.3432**
M64	.4157**	.4945**	.3432**	1.0000
V21	-.1054	-.0995	-.0033	.0503
V16	-.1963**	-.0896	.0209	-.0405
AGEMAR	.2438**	.2170**	.0737	.0752
MARDUR	-.3721**	-.3490**	.1246	-.0493
BOTHMOVE	.1447*	.0951	.0580	.0835
WIFEMOVE	-.0091	-.0474	.0407	-.0022
HUSBMOVE	-.1152	-.1052	-.1191	-.1512*
LONGMAR	-.3372**	-.3013**	.0810	-.0532
SHORTMAR	.3136**	.3026**	-.1482*	.0301

	BOTHMOVE	WIFEMOVE	HUSBMOVE·
V45	.0436	.0642	.0031
V44	.0669	.0614	-.0856
V43	-.0222	.0772	-.0603
V38	-.0188	-.0240	.0420
V36	.0062	-.0170	.0354
V66	-.0193	.0675	-.0547
V8	.1447*	-.0091	-.1152
M8	.0951	-.0474	-.1052
V64	.0580	.0407	-.1191
M64	.0835	-.0022	-.1512*
V21	-.0108	-.0444	.0369
V16	-.0776	.0347	-.0075
AGEMAR	-.0283	.0181	-.0742
MARDUR	-.0031	-.0241	.0484
BOTHMOVE	1.0000	-.5676**	-.4139**
WIFEMOVE	-.5676**	1.0000	-.3282**
HUSBMOVE	-.4139**	-.3282**	1.0000
LONGMAR	-.0660	-.0407	.0858
SHORTMAR	.0326	-.0015	-.0688

	AGEMAR	MARDUR	LONGMAR	SHORTMAR
V45	.0088	-.2149**	-.2791**	.1984**
V44	-.0224	-.2408**	-.2833**	.2298**
V43	-.0674	.2472**	.2003**	-.1736*
V38	.0485	-.5452**	-.3274**	.4785**
V36	-.2259**	.7099**	.4884**	-.6135**
V66	-.0539	.0413	.0404	.0161
V8	.2438**	-.3721**	-.3372**	.3136**
M8	.2170**	-.3490**	-.3013**	.3026**
V64	.0737	.1246	.0810	-.1482*
M64	.0752	-.0493	-.0532	.0301
V21	-.1244	.1198	.0742	-.1069
V16	.2652**	.0473	-.0046	-.0969
AGEMAR	1.0000	-.3785**	-.3668**	.2030**
MARDUR	-.3785**	1.0000	.7838**	-.8419**
BOTHMOVE	-.0283	-.0031	-.0660	.0326
WIFEMOVE	.0181	-.0241	-.0407	-.0015
HUSBMOVE	-.0742	.0484	.0858	-.0688
LONGMAR	-.3668**	.7838**	1.0000	-.5588**
SHORTMAR	.2030**	-.8419**	-.5588**	1.0000

Variables in Matrix:

Mardur = Duration of marriage
Agemar = Age at marriage
V66 = Resource control decision (wife)
V45 = Ever-use contraception
V44 = Frequency of family planning discussion
V43 = Ideal family size
V38 = Desire for addittional children
V36 = CEB
V8 = Wife's educationlits with husband's mother
M8 = Husband's education
V7 = Wife's age
M7 = Husband's Age
V21 = Urban - rural residence
V16 = Union order
Bothmove = Both spouses moved
Wifemove = Only wife moved
Longmar = Married 26+ years
Shortmar = Married 15 or fewer years
V64 = Wife's income
M64 = Husband's income

Bibliography

Afshar, H. 1985. "Introduction," in Afshar (ed.), *Women, Work, and Ideology in the Third World*, Tabistock Publications, New York.

Anker, Richard 1982. "Demographic Change and the Role of Women: A Research Programme in Developing Countries," in Richard Anker, Mayra Buvinic and Nadia H. Youssef (eds.), *Women's Roles and Population Trends in the Third World*, Croom Helm, London, pp.239-267.

Arizpe, L. 1981. "Relay Migration and the Survival of the Peasant Household," in J. Balan (ed.), *Why People Move*, UNESCO, pp.187-209.

Arndt, H.W. 1983. "The Trickle-Down Myth," *Economic Development and Cultural Change*, 32(1), pp.1-10.

Ariffin, J. 1984. "Migration of Women Workers in Peninsular Malaysia: Impact and Implications," in J.T. Fawcett et al. (eds.), *Women in the Cities of Asia*, Westview Press, Boulder, CO, pp. 213-226.

Arnold, F. and S. Piampiti, 1984. "Female Migration in Thailand," in J.T. Fawcett et al. (eds.), *Women in the Cities of Asia*, Westview Press, Boulder, CO, pp. 143-164.

Bangun, M. 1981. "Functional Education and Credit Facilities," in T.S. Epstein and R.A. Watts (eds.), *The Endless Day: Some Case Material on Asian Rural Women*, Pergamon Press, New York, pp.128-154.

Bauer, J. 1984. "New Models and Traditional Networks: Migrant Women in Tehran," J.T. Fawcett et al. (eds.), *Women in the Cities of Asia*, Westview Press, Boulder, CO, pp.269-296.

144

Beckman, L.J. 1983. "Communication, Power, and the Influence of Social Networks in Couple Decisions on Fertility," in R.A. Bulatoao and R.D Lee (eds.), *Determinants of Fertility in Developing Countries: Fertility Regulation and Institutional Influences,* Volume 2, Academic Press, New York, pp.415-443.

Birdsall, Nancy 1980. "Population Growth and Poverty in the Developing World," *Population Bulletin,* 35 (5).

Birdsall, N. and W.P. Mc Greevey 1983. "Women, Poverty and Development," in M.Buvinic, M.A. Lycette, and W.P. McGreevey (eds.), *Women and Poverty in the Third World,* Johns Hopkins University Press, Baltimore, pp.3-13.

Boserup, E. 1970. *Woman's Role in Economic Development,* St. Martin's Press, New York.

Brown, Lester R. 1981. "World Food Resources and Population: the Narrowing Margin," *Population Bulletin,* 36 (3).

Bryceson, D. F. 1985. "Women's Proletarianization and the Family Wage in Tanzania," in Afshar (ed.), *Women, Work, and Ideology in the Third World,* Tavistock Publications, New York.

Byerlee, D., J.L. Tommy, and H. Fatoo, 1977. "Rural-urban Migration in Sierra Leone: Determinants and Policy Implications," *African Rural Economy Paper No. 13,* Dept. of Agricultural Economics, Njala University College and Michigan State University.

Cain, M. 1984. *On Women's Status, Family Structure, and Fertility in Developing Countries,* Center for Policy Studies: The Population Council, New York.

Caldwell, J.C. 1980. "Mass Education as a Determinant of the Timing of Fertility Decline," Population and Development Review, 6(2) pp.225-255.

Caldwell, J.C. 1976. "Toward a Restatement of the Demographic Transition Theory," *Population and Development Review*, 2(3-4), pp.321-366.

Caldwell, J.C., Reddy, P.H., and Caldwell, P. 1983. "The Causes of Marriage in South India," *Population Studies*, 37(3), pp.343-362.

Casterline, J.W., L.W. Williams, and P.F. McDonald. 1986. The Age Difference Between Spouses: Variations among Developing Countries, *Population Studies*, 40, pp.353-374.

Castro, M.G. and Z.L.C. Oliveira. 1978. "Migrant Women: the Role of Labor Mobility in the Process of Production and Reproduction," *Paper Prepared for the International Labor Organization Role of Women and Demographic Change Research Programme*, Geneva, Switzerland.

Chaudhury, R.H. 1978. "Determinants and Consequences of Rural Out-Migration: Evidence from Some Villages in Bangladesh," *Economic and Demographic Change: Issues for the 1980's*, Proceedings of the 1978 ISUUP Conference held in Helsinki, ISUUP, Belguim, pp.213-228.

Cheung, P.; J. Cabigon, A. Chamratrithirong, P.F. McDonald, S. Syed, A. Cherlin, and P. Smith 1985. "Cultural Variations in the Transition to Marriage in Four Asian Societies," in *International Population Conference/ Congres International de la Population*, Florence 1985, 5-12 June/juin, vol. 3, International Union for the Scientific Study of Population (IUSSP), Liege, Belgium, pp. 293-308.

Chilivumbo, A. 1985. *Migration and Uneven Rural Development in Africa: The Case of Zambia*, University Press of America, Lanham, MD.

Cochrane, S.H. 1983. "Effects of Education and Urbanization on Fertility," in R.A. Bulatao and R.D. Lee (eds.), *Determinants of Fertility in Developing Countries*, Volume 2, Academic Press, New York, pp. 587-626.

146

Cochrane, S.H.   1979.   *Fertility and Education: What Do We Really Know?*   Johns Hopkins University Press, Baltimore.

Conklin, G.H.   1981. "Cultural Determinants of Power for Women Within the Family: A Neglected Aspect of Family Research," in G. Kurian and R. Ghosh, *Women in the Family and the Economy: An International Comparative Study*, Greenwood Press, Westport, CT, pp.9-27.

Connell, J.   1984.   "Status or Sub???   Women, Migration and Development in the South   Pacific," *International Migration Review*, 18 (4), pp. 964-983.

Connell, J. and M. Lipton,   1977. *Assessing Village Labour Situations in Developing Countries*, Oxford   University Press, Delhi.

Connell, J., B. Dasgupta, R. Laishley and M. Lipton.   1976.   *Migration from Rural Areas*, Oxford University Press, Oxford.

Curtin, L.B.   1982.   *Status of Women: A Comparative Analysis of Twenty Developing Countries*, Population Reference Bureau, Washington.

de Oliveira, O. and B. Garcia.   1984.   "Urbanization, Migration and the Growth of Large Cities: Trends   and Implications in Some Developing Countries," in *Population Distribution, Migration and Development: Proceedings of the   Expert Group on Population Distribution, Migration and Development*, Hammamet (Tunsia), 21-25 March 1983, United Nations, New York.

Dixon, R.B.   1971.   "Explaining Cross-Cultural Variations in Age at Marriage and   Proportions Never Marrying," *Population Studies*, 25,   pp.215-230.

Dixon, R.B.   1975.   "Women's Rights, Family Planning and Family Size: An International Perspective," in Gladys Gary Vaughn (ed.), *Women's Roles and Education: Changing Traditions in Population Planning*, American Home Economics Association, Washington, D.C.

Dixon, R.B. 1978.   *Rural Woman at Work,* John Hopkins University Press, Baltimore.

147

Duley, M.I. and S. Diduk. 1986. "Women, Colonialism, and Development," in M.I. Duley and M.I. Edwards, *The Cross-Cultural Study of Women: A Comprehensive Guide*, The Feminist Press, New York, pp.48-77.

Dyson, T., and M. Moore 1983. "Kinship Structure, Female Autonomy, and Demographic Behavior in India," *Population and Development Review*, 9(1), pp.35-60.

Epstein, T.S. 1981. "Rural Women and Their Multiple Roles," in T.S. Epstein and R.A. Watts, (eds.) *The Endless Day: Some Case Material on Asian Rural Women*, Pergamon Press, New York, pp.157-167.

Eviota, E.V. and P.C. Smith. 1984. "The Migration of Women in the Philippines," in *Women in the Cities of Asia*, J.T. Fawcett et al. (eds.), Westview Press, Boulder, CO, pp. 165-190.

Fawcett, J., S.E. Khoo, and P.C. Smith. 1984. "Urbanization, Migration, and the Status of Women," in J.T. Fawcett et al. (eds.), *Women in the Cities of Asia*, Westview Press, Boulder, CO, pp. 3-14.

Fields, G.S. 1979. "Lifetime Migration in Colombia," *Economic Development and Cultural Change*, 30(3), pp.539-558.

Findley, S. 1977. *Planning for Internal Migration: A Review of Issues and Policies in Developing Countries*, U.S. Bureau of the Census, ISP-RD-4, U.S. Government Printing Office, Washington, D.C.

Findley, S. and L. Williams 1987. *Women Who Go and Women Who Stay: Twin Reflections of Family Migration Processes in a Changing World*, unpublished manuscript.

Freedman, R., S.E. Khoo, and B. Supraptilah. 1981. "Modern Contraceptive Use in Indonesia: A Challenge to Conventional Wisdom," *Scientific Reports*, (20), World Fertility Survey, London.

Gardet, L. 1954. *La Cite Musulmane: Vie Sociale et Politique* (The Muslim City: Social and Political Life).

Geertz, H. 1961. *The Javanese Family*, The Free Press of Glencoe, Inc., New York.

Goldscheider, C. 1983. "The Adjustment of Migrants in Large
    Cities of Less Developed Countries," in C.
    Goldscheider (ed.), *Urban Migrants in Developing
    Nations*, Westview, Boulder, pp.233-254.

Goldscheider, C. 1984. "Comparative Perspectives on Rural
    Migration and Development," in C. Goldscheider (ed),
    Rural Migration in Developing Nations. Westview,
    Boulder,
    pp 289-308.

Goldstein, S. 1973. "Interrelations Between Migration and
    Fertility in Thailand," *Demography*, 10(2), pp.225-242.

Goldstein, S. and P. Tirasawat. 1977. *The Fertility of
    Migrants to Urban Places in Thailand*, East-West
    Population Institute, Honolulu.

Goode, W.J. 1982. *The Family*, Prentice-Hall, Inc.,
    Englewood Cliffs, NJ.

Goode, W.J. 1963. *World Revolution and Family Patterns*,
    The Free Press of Glencoe, New York, NY.

Guest, M.P. 1987. *Labor Allocation and Mobility in Four
    Villages in Central Java*, unpublished dissertation,
    Brown University, Providence, RI.

Gugler, J. 1982. "Overurbanization Reconsidered,"
    Economic Development and Cultural Change, 31(1),
    pp.173-189.

Hafkin, N.J. and E.G. Bay 1976. "Introduction", in Hafkin,
    N.J. and E.G. Bay (eds.), *Women in Africa*, Stanford
    University Press, Stanford, pp. 1-18.

Herold, J. 1979. "Female Migration in Chile: Types of
    Moves and Socioeconomic Characteristics," *Demography*,
    16(2), pp. 257-277.

Hollerbach, P.E. 1983. "Fertility Decision-Making
    Processes: A Critical Essay," in R.A. Bulateo and R.D.
    Lee (eds.), *Determinants of Fertility in Developing
    Countries: Fertility Regulation and Institutional
    Influences*, Vol. 2, Academic Press, New York.

Huang, N.C. 1984. "The Migration of Rural Women to Taipei," in J.T. Fawcett et al. (eds.), *Women in the Cities of Asia*. Westview Press, Boulder, CO, pp. 247-268.

Hugo, G. 1982. "Circular Migration in Indonesia," *Population and Development Review*, 8(1), pp.59-83.

Hugo, G. 1981. "Implications of the Imbalance in Age and Sex Composition of Sub-Areas as a Consequence of Migration: The Case of a Rural Developing Nation-Indonesia," International Population Conference: Solicited Papers, Vol. 2, International Union for the Scientific Study of Population (IUSSP), Leige, Belgium, pp. 387-415.

Hull, T.H. 1981. "The 'Positive Relation' and Future Indonesian Fertility," *Research Note* prepared for the International Population Dynamics Program, Department of Demography, The Australian National University, Canberra.

Hull, V. 1976. *Women in Java's Rural Middle Class: Progress or Regress?* Population Institute, Gajah Mada University, Jogjakarta, Indonesia, unpublished manuscript.

Hull, T.H. and V.J. Hull 1984. "Population Change in Indonesia: Findings of the 1980 Census," *Bulletin of Indonesian Economic Studies*, 20(3), pp.95-117.

Ihromi, T.O., M.G.Tan, J.Rahardjo, M.Wanjudi, S.Djuarini, A.Djahri, 1973. *The Status of Women and Family Planning in Indonesia*, Indonesian Planned Parenthood Association, Research and Evaluation Division, National Training and Research Center.

Indonesia, Biro Pusat Statistik. 1983. *Data Hasil Pendaftaran Rumah Tangga*, Kantor Statistik, Kabupaten Sukoharjo, Sukoharjo.

Indonesia, Biro Pusat Statistik. 1982. *Penduduk Indonesia*, (Results of the Sub-sample of the 1980 Population Census), Seri S (1), Preliminary Tables, Biro Pusat Statistik, Jakarta, Indonesia.

Indonesia, Biro Pusat Statistik. 1980. *Penduduk Kabupaten Sukoharjo 1980*, Hasil Pencacahan Lengkap, Biro Pusat Statistik, Kantor Statistik Kabupaten Sukoharjo, Propinsi Jawa Tengah.

Indonesia, Department of Information. 1968. *The Indonesian Women Movement: A Chronological Survey of the Women Movement in Indonesia*, Department of Information, Republic of Indonesia, Jakarta.

International Migration Review. 1984. Full Issue, 18 (4).

Jay, R.R. 1969. *Javanese Villagers: Social Relations in Rural Modjokuto*, The MIT Press, Cambridge, MA.

Jelin, Elizabeth. 1982. "Women and the Urban Labour Market," in Richard Anker, Mayra Buvinic and Nadia H. Youssef (eds.), *Women's Roles and Population Trends in the Third World*. Croom Helm, London, pp.239-267.

Khoo, S.E. and P. Pirie. 1984. "Female Rural-to-Urban Migration in Peninsular Malaysia," in J.T. Fawcett et al. (eds.), *Women in the Cities of Asia*, Westview Press, Boulder, CO, pp. 125-142.

Knodel, J. and E. van de Walle. 1979. "Lessons from the Past: Policy Implications of Historical Fertility Studies," *Population and Development Review*, 5(2), pp.217-245.

Knotts, M.A. 1977. *The Social and Economic Factors Associated With The Rural-Urban Migration of Kenyan Women*, unpublished Ph.D. Dissertation, Johns Hopkins University, Baltimore.

Koentjaraningrat. 1967. "Tjelapar: A Village in South Central Java," in *Villages in Indonesia*, Cornell University Press: Ithaca.

Lee, E. 1966. "A Theory of Migration," *Demography*, 3 (1), pp. 47-57.

Leiserson, M., B.Swadesh, C.Chandrasekaran, D.Chernichovsky, R.Key, O.A.Meesook, and P.Suebsaeng. 1980. *Indonesia: Employment and Income Distribution in Indonesia*, The World Bank, Washington, D.C.

151

Lightfoot, P. T. Fuller, and P. Ramnuansilpa. 1982.
"Circulation and Interpersonal Networks Linking Rural
and Urban Areas: The Case of Roi-Et, Northeastern
Thailand," *East West Institute Paper 84*, Honolulu, HI

Lipman-Blumen, J. 1984. *Gender Roles and Power*, Prentice-
Hall, Inc., Englewood Cliffs, NJ.

Lipton, M. 1982. "Migration from Rural Areas: The Impact
of Rural Productivity and Income Distribution," in
*Migration and the Labor Market in Developing
Countries*, Westview Press, Boulder.

Little, K. 1973. *African Women in Towns*, Cambridge
University Press, Cambridge.

Malthus, Thomas R. 1959. *Population: The First Essay*,
University of Michigan Press, Ann Arbor, MI,
(originally published in 1798).

Mangkuprawira, S. 1981. "Married Women's Work Pattern in
Rural Java," in T.S. Epstein and R.A. Watts, (eds.),
*The Endless Day: Some Case Material on Asian Rural
Women*, Pergamon Press, New York, pp.84-106.

Mann, Michael. 1986. "A Crisis in Stratification Theory?"
in Rosemary Crompton and Michael Mann (eds.), *Gender
and Stratification*, Polity Press, New York, pp. 40-56.

Martine, G. 1979. "Adaption of Migrants or Survival of the
Fittest? A Brazilian Case," *Journal of Developing
Areas*, 14(1), pp. 23-41.

Mason, K.O. 1971. *Social and Economic Correlates of
Family Fertility: A Survey of the Evidence*, Research
Triangle Institute, North Carolina.

Mason, K.O. 1985. *The Status of Women: A Review of its
Relationships to Fertility and Mortality*, The
Rockefellar Foundation, New York, NY.

Mather, C. 1985. "'Rather Than Make Trouble, It's Better
Just to Leave': Behind the Lack of Industrial Strife
in the Tangerang Region of West Java," in Afshar
(ed.), *Women, Work, and Ideology in the Third World*,
Tavistock Publications, New York.

Mazur, R.E. 1984. "Rural Out-Migration and Labor Allocation in Mali," in C. Goldscheider (ed.), *Rural Migration in Developing Nations*, Westview, Boulder, CO. pp. 209-288.

Meek, Ronald. 1971. *Marx and Engels and the Population Bomb*, The Ramparts Press.

Merriam-Webster. 1974. *Webster's New Collegiate Dictionary*, G. and C. Merriam Co., Springfield, MA.

McNicoll, G. and M. Singarimbun. 1983. *Fertility Decline in Indonesia: Analysis and Interpretation*, National Academy Press, Washington, DC.

Mueller, E. 1983. "Measuring Women's Poverty in Developing Countries," in M. Buvinic, M.A. Lycette, and W.P. McGreevey (eds.), *Women and Poverty in the Third World*, Johns Hopkins University Press, Baltimore, MD. pp. 272-285.

Mueller, E. and K. Short. 1983. "Effects of Income and Wealth on the Demand for Children," in R.A. Bulateo and R.D. Lee (eds.), *Determinants of Fertility in Developing Countries: Supply and Demand for Children*, Vol. 1, Academic Press, New York.

Murray, C. 1981. *Families Divided: The Impact of Migration in Lesotho*, African Studies Series No. 29, Cambridge University Press, Cambridge.

Nag, M., N.F. White, R.C. Peet. 1980. "An Anthropological Approach to the Study of the Economic Value of Children in Java and Nepal," in H.P.Binswanger et al. (eds.), *Rural Household Studies in Asia*, Singapore University Press, pp. 248-288.

National Research Council. 1986. *Population Growth and Economic Development: Policy Questions*, National Academy Press, Washington, D.C.

Oppong, C. 1982. "Family Structure and Women's Reproductive and Productive Roles: Some Conceptual and Methodological Issues," in R. Anker, M. Buvinic and N.H. Yousef (eds.). *Women's Roles and Population Trends in the Third World*, Croom Helm, London.

Palmier, L.H. 1960. *Social Status and Power in Java*, The Athlone Press, London.

Parsons, J.S. 1984. "What Makes the Indonesian Family Planning Programme Tick," *POPULI*, 11(3), pp. 5-19.

Piampiti, S. 1984. "Female Migrants in Bangkok Metropolis," in J.T. Fawcett et al. (eds.), *Women in the Cities of Asia*, Westview Press, Boulder, CO, pp. 247-268.

Population Reference Bureau. *1984 World Population Data Sheet*, the Population Reference Bureau, Inc., Washington, D.C.

Powers, M. 1985. "Measuring the Situation of Women from Existing Data," *Paper prepared for the Rockefellar Foundation's Workshop on Women's Status and Fertility*, Mount Kisco, NY.

Pusat Jaringan Informasi & Dokumentasi Program KB Nasional. 1985. *Kumpulan Data: Kependudukan & Kiluarga Berencana Indonesia*, Badan Koordinasi Keluarga Berencana Nasional, Jakarta, Indonesia.

Ranney, S. and S. Kossoudji. 1983. "Profiles of Temporary Mexican Labor Migrants to the United States," *Population and Development Review*, 9(3), pp. 475-493.

Ravenstein, E.G. 1885. "The Laws of Migration," *Journal of the Statistical Society*, 48(2), pp. 167-235.

Rindfuss, R. and P. Morgan. 1983. "Marriage, Sex, and the First Birth Interval in Asia," *Population and Development Review*, 9(2), pp. 259-278.

Sabot, R.H. 1979. *Economic Development and Urban Migration*, Clarendon Press, Oxford.

Sadik, Nafis. 1984. *Population: The UNFPA Experience*, New York University Press, New York.

Safilios-Rothschild, C. 1982. "Female Power, Autonomy and Demographic Change in the Third World," in R. Anker, M. Buvinic and N. H. Youssef (eds.), *Women's Roles and Population Trends in the Third World*, Croom Helm, London.

Shah, N. 1984. "The Female Migrant in Pakistan," in J.T. Fawcett et al., (eds.), *Women in the Cities of Asia*, Westview Press, Boulder, CO, pp. 208-124.

Shaw, R.P. 1975. *Migration Theory and Fact*, Regional Science Research Institute, Philadelphia.

Shryock, H.S., Jr. 1964. *Population Mobility Within the United States*, Community and Family Study Center, University of Chicago, Chicago.

Simon, Julian. 1977. *The Economics of Population Growth*, Princeton University Press, Princeton, NJ

Singh, A.M. 1984. "Rural-to-Urban Migration of Women in India: Patterns and Implications," in J.T. Fawcett et al. (eds.), *Women in the Cities of Asia*, Westview Press, Boulder, CO, pp. 81-107.

Smelser, N. 1968. "Toward a Theory of Modernization," in *Essays in Sociological Explanation*, Prentice Hall: Englewood Cliffs, NJ, pp. 125-147.

Smith, P.C. 1980. "Asian Marriage Patterns in Transition," *Journal of Family History*, 5(1), pp. 58-96.

Smith, P.C. 1982. *Contrasting Marriage Patterns and Fertility in Southeast Asia: Indonesian and the Philippines Compared*, East-West Center, Honolulu, HI.

Smith, P.C. 1981. *Migration, Sex, and Occupations in Urban Indonesia and Thailand*, Papers of the East-West Population Institute, #139, Honolulu.

Smith, P.C. and M.S. Karim. 1980. *Urbanization, Education, and Marriage Patterns: Four Cases from Asia*, Papers of the East-West Population Institute, #70, Honolulu.

Soon, Y.S.Y. 1977. "The Role of Korean Women in National Development," in S. Mattielli (ed.), *Virtues in Conflict, Royal Asiatic Society*, Soeul, Korea, pp. 157-167.

Speare, A., Jr. and J. Harris 1986. "Education, Earnings and Migration in Indonesia," *Economic Development and Cultural Change*, 34(2), pp. 223-244.

Standing, H. 1985. "Resources, Wages, and Power: the Impact of Women's Employment on the Urban Bengali Household," in Afshar (ed.), *Women, Work, and Ideology in the Third World*, Tavistock Publications, New York.

Staudt, K.A. 1982. "Women Farmers and Inequites in Agricultural Services," in E.G. Bay, (ed.), *Women and Work in Africa*, Westview, Boulder, pp. 207-224.

Stivens, M. 1985. "The Fate of Women's Land Rights: Gender, Matriliny, and Capitalism in Rembau, Negeri Sembilan, Malaysia," in Afshar (ed.), *Women, Work, and Ideology in the Third World*, Tavistock Publications, New York.

Stone, L. 1977. *The Family, Sex and Marriage in England: 1500-1800*, Harper and Row, New York.

Suparlan, P. and H. Sigit. 1980. *Culture and Fertility: The Case of Indonesia*, Research Notes and Discussion Paper No. 18, The Institute of Southeast Asian Studies, Singapore.

Taylor, D. 1985. "Women: An Analysis," in *Women: A World Report*, Oxford University Press, New York.

Teachman, J. 1979. "Evaluation of the Impact of Family Planning on Java's Birth Rate," in *The Impact of Family Planning Programs on Fertility Rates: A Case Study of Four Nations*, University of Chicago Press, Chicago, pp. 86-128.

Thadani, V.N. 1978. "The Logic of Sentiment: The Family and Social Change," *Population and Development Review*, 4(3), pp. 457-499.

Thadani, V.N. and M.P. Todaro. 1984. "Female Migration: A Conceptual Framework," in J.T. Fawcett et al. (eds.), *Women in the Cities of Asia*, Westview Press, Boulder, CO, pp. 36-59.

Thadani, V.N. and M.P. Todaro. 1979. *Female Migration in Developing Countries: A Framework for Analysis*, Center for Policy Studies Working Paper No. 47, Population Council, New York.

United Nations. 1981. *Migration, Urbanization and Development in Indonesia*, ESCAP, Bangkok.

United Nations Secretariat. 1984. "General Overview," *Fertility and Family, Proceedings of the Expert Group on Fertility and Family*, New Delhi, 5-11 January 1983: United Nations, New York.

Van der Tak, Jean; Carl Haub and Elaine Murphy. 1979. "Our Population Predicament: A New Look," *Population Bulletin* 34(5).

Vreede-de Stuers, C. 1960. *The Indonesian Woman: Struggles and Achievements*, Mouton and Co., the Hague, Netherlands.

Ware, H. 1978. *The Economic Value of Children in Asia and Africa: Comparative Perspectives*, Papers of the East-West Population Institute, #50, Honolulu.

Ware, H. 1981. *Women, Demography, and Development*, The Australian National University, Canberra.

Warner, R.L., G.R. Lee, and J. Lee. 1986. "Social Organization, Spousal Resources, and Marital Power: A Cross-cultural Study," *Journal of Marriage and the Family* (48) pp. 121-128.

Warwick, D.P. 1986. "The Indonesian Family Planning Program: Government Influence and Client Choice," *Population and Development Review*, 12(3), pp. 453-490.

White, B.N.F. 1976. *Production and Reproduction in a Javanese Village*, unpublished PhD dissertation, The Agricultural Development Council, Bogor, Indonesia.

Whyte, M.K. 1978. *The Status of Women in Preindustrial Societies*, Princeton University Press, Princeton, NJ.

Whyte, R.O. and P. Whyte. 1982. *The Women of Rural Asia*, Westview Press, Boulder, CO.

Williams, L. and P. Guest. 1985. *Female Status as a Determinant of Contraceptive Use*, Paper presented at the 1985 meetings of the Population Association of America, March 28-30, Boston, MA.

World Bank. 1984. *World Development Report* 1984, Oxford University Press, New York, NY.

Yap, L. 1976. "Rural-Urban Migration and Urban Underemployment in Brazil," *Journal of Development Economics*, 3(3), pp. 227-243.

Yousef, N.H. 1982. "The Interrelationship Between the Division of Labour in the Household, Women's Roles and Their Impact on Fertility," in R. Anker, M. Buvinic and N.H. Youssef (eds.), *Women's Roles and Population Trends in the Third World*, Croom Helm, London.

Yousef, N., M. Buvinic, and A. Kudat. 1979. *Women in Migration: A Third World Focus*, Agency for International Development, Washington.